The Making *of a* Biblical Leader

The Making *of a* Biblical Leader

ROBERT L. FURROW

General Editor

HARVEST HOUSE PUBLISHERS

EUGENE, OREGON

Cover design by Studio Gearbox

Cover image © HomeArt / Shutterstock

Interior design by KUHN Design Group

For bulk, special sales, or ministry purchases, please call 1-800-547-8979.
Email: CustomerService@hhpbooks.com

The Making of a Biblical Leader
Copyright © 2025 by Robert L. Furrow / General Editor
Published by Harvest House Publishers
Eugene, Oregon 97408
www.harvesthousepublishers.com

ISBN 978-0-7369-9150-6 (pbk)
ISBN 978-0-7369-9151-3 (eBook)

Library of Congress Control Number: 2024947380

Printed in the United States of America

25 26 27 28 29 30 31 32 33 / BP / 10 9 8 7 6 5 4 3 2 1

To my wife, Kathy.

You not only put up with my endless hours of overworking with much-needed patience, but also bravely faced my grammar with your editing expertise. Thank you for your dedication and grace, considering the manuscript deadline fell on your birthday. Your perseverance, wisdom, and love made this book possible and far more readable.

Thank you for your belief in me and for making this journey one we face together.

ACKNOWLEDGMENTS

I want to extend my deepest gratitude to the incredible team of authors who contributed to this book: Frank Turek, Gary Hamrick, Skip Heitzig, Lenya Heitzig, David Guzik, Daniel Fusco, Sean McDowell, Ed Taylor, and Jim Gallagher—your wisdom, dedication, and insight have brought much depth, clarity, and truth to these pages, and I am truly honored to have worked alongside you. A special thank you to Tyler Akin for his work on the original transcripts and to Lyle Steffens for his editing assistance. I also want to express my sincere appreciation to Jessica Balanda for her excellent coordinative efforts and dedication in bringing this project together. A heartfelt thank you, as well, to Bob Hawkins and the outstanding staff at Harvest House Publishers for their encouragement, thoughtful insights, careful attention to detail, and commitment to excellence. I especially want to thank my wife, Kathy, whose diligent work, keen eye, patience, wisdom, and unwavering support have been an essential part of this process. Thank you to everyone for your hard work, your faithfulness, and your commitment to the truth. I am deeply grateful.

CONTENTS

FOREWORD

Erwin W. Lutzer

If I could choose just one book to read on the topic of biblical leadership, this would be it.

When I read the first chapter of this book, "Good and Bad Leaders" by Robert Furrow, I was convinced this chapter alone is worth the price of the book. I also wished I had this book to read when I was a young pastor so many years ago. As I continued to read the rest of the chapters, each written by a different contributor, I became convinced that not only was this book biblical, it was also practical and realistic.

Nothing happens without leadership, whether the leader is good, bad, or somewhere in between. No matter where a leader lands on the scale, they will have a disproportionate impact on those whom they lead. Though we often hear stories of failed leaders, we need to hold before us examples of what faithful leadership looks like.

So, yes, this book lives up to its title. It is a book on *biblical leadership*, not a list of lessons drawn from the corporate world, not a formula for how to get to the top, nor how to accumulate power. Instead, it's a book on how to lead through relationships, how to maintain earned respect, and how to lead with a spirit of servanthood.

The Making of a Biblical Leader deals with the character of a leader: from integrity and a commitment to truth to having a heart for the hurting. It reminds us that leadership should never be taken for granted or used for personal gain. It warns about "lording it over a flock" and setting ourselves apart from the struggles of the common person.

The contributors to this book know that leadership is a calling, not a right. We've all known leaders who acted as if their followers belonged to them. Consider the contrast between Saul and David, whose stories are told in considerable detail in the Old Testament. Saul clung to his leadership even when God had taken it from him; he clung until his knuckles turned white, and apparently died by suicide. After David sinned and eventually had to leave Jerusalem, he left his future leadership entirely in God's hands. He knew the kingdom was not his to keep.

Recently, I spoke in a thriving church whose building was donated to them by a previous congregation that closed its doors because it couldn't survive in their changing neighborhood. I asked myself: How come this church was growing in the very building where another church couldn't survive? I soon discovered the answer: The pastor modeled biblical leadership.

Now for a very personal word: There are some books on leadership that emphasize the personality of the leader, who is expected to be dynamic, decisive, and visionary, all wrapped up in a bundle of multiple gifts. Those kinds of books are a discouragement to me personally. What I need is a book for the ordinary leader, for the person who has no extraordinary gifts but still feels the call of God on their life.

The Making of a Biblical Leader stresses that character is more important than gifting, and humility is more important than being a "super leader." This book is for the ordinary man or woman who can thoughtfully share their heart with people, who can enlist others who make up for their own weaknesses, and who doesn't care who gets the credit for what God does.

Read this book, share it with the leaders in your orbit, and realize that good biblical leadership does not come automatically: God gives us gifts of leadership, but these skills need to be honed and developed—and God promises to enable all those whom He calls.

Erwin W. Lutzer
Pastor Emeritus
The Moody Church, Chicago

PART 1

THE ESSENTIALS

CHAPTER 1

GOOD AND BAD LEADERS

Robert Furrow

Armed with my newly earned B+ from a high school elective auto upholstery class, I marched down to the nearest auto upholstery shop and filled out a job application. I was hired on the spot! The extent of my experience was that I had spent about an hour a day during a sophomore semester learning the ins and outs of how to be a trimmer, otherwise known as one who restores the insides of automobiles.

What did I quickly learn? I was woefully unprepared for the work I was hired to do. I spent the next six months after school taking seats out of cars, cutting off the old seat covers, watching someone else make new seat covers, installing the new seat covers that someone else had sewn, and reinstalling the seats. It was clear that my high school class had not prepared me as a trimmer.

Fast-forward about seven years. I'm now the pastor of a church plant in Tucson, Arizona, that has experienced steady growth. We've moved into our first rented building, which holds about 300 people, and we have two services on Sunday morning. All the basics are in place to run the church successfully. We have a good worship team, a plan to teach through the Bible, a great Sunday school director and teachers, and more.

What did I quickly learn? I was woefully unprepared for the work I was called to do. The problem was not in what we were doing as a church, but in the intricacies of leadership. I wasn't unfamiliar with leadership theory, but I had yet to discover the principles of biblical leadership. The chasm between secular and biblical leadership theory reminded me of the difference between a seasoned trimmer and a sophomore who completed an auto upholstery class. Many in the church have similar misunderstandings about leadership, not realizing that leadership among Christians is different.

Take, for example, the time James and John brought their mother to Jesus. She asked if her sons could sit at His right hand and left in His kingdom. Jesus asked James and John if they were able drink the cup He was about to drink and be baptized with the baptism that He would be baptized with. They answered with great exuberance, "We are able," being entirely unaware that Jesus was referring to His future suffering. When the other disciples heard of this power move, they were angry. Jesus called them together, teaching them that greatness and leadership are different among Christians.

> Jesus called them to Himself and said, "You know that the rulers of the Gentiles lord it over them, and those who are great exercise authority over them. Yet it shall not be so among you; but whoever desires to become great among you, let him be your servant. And whoever desires to be first among you, let him be your slave—just as the Son of Man did not come to be served, but to serve, and to give His life a ransom for many" (Matthew 20:25-28).

Note a few key differences here for those who are in biblical leadership positions. They…

- do not lord over those they lead
- do not exercise authority over those they lead
- serve those they lead
- are even slaves to those they lead

This gives us insight into the kind of Christ-directed leadership we will explore in this book.

WHAT IS LEADERSHIP?

The first and simplest definition of a leader is "one who leads the way" or "one who goes first." In that sense, all of us are involved in leadership. You don't need an office, a title, or a position to lead. For every observable action we take, it is possible that another person will take notice and adjust their actions accordingly. Whether we're a corporate executive officer, manager, teacher, laborer, parent, or an older sibling, our attitudes and actions directly affect the future and success of the people we lead.

THE UNIQUE CALL FOR CHRISTIANS

Even if you think you're not a leader, the fact that you're a Christian puts you in a leadership role. When we come to Christ, we receive a calling to set an example and lead others to the truth of Christ, being an ambassador or representative of God wherever we go. Read what the Bible says about those who are in Christ: "Now then, we are ambassadors for Christ, as though God were pleading through us: we implore you on Christ's behalf, be reconciled to God" (2 Corinthians 5:20).

Considering that other people's temporal and eternal outcomes depend, in part, on our leadership, it's wise to learn what we can about leading well and developing the qualities that will lead to success.

WHY BIBLICAL LEADERSHIP?

There are all kinds of leadership theories in use today that remain in a constant state of flux. If we want to grow in our leadership abilities, there is a never-ending supply of resources—books, articles, podcasts, subscriptions, leadership coaches and groups, video classes, etc. For the most part, we can apply the lessons from these resources and become a better leader. However, there is one resource that has been around for 2,000-plus years and is unique in its teaching to leaders. The Scriptures have provided direction to millions of people on how we are to live and lead. Consider what we have in the gift of Scripture:

> All Scripture is given by inspiration of God, and is profitable for doctrine, for reproof, for correction, for instruction in righteousness, that the man of God may be complete, thoroughly equipped for every good work (2 Timothy 3:16-17).

Biblical leadership is not limited solely to spiritual leadership, nor is it limited to the church. It is extremely useful to all Christians who are in a leadership capacity of any kind. If you're a Christian and you manage a business or lead in any other way, biblical leadership will contribute to your success—for several reasons. Here's why:

First, the Scriptures are inspired. I don't mean inspired like a magazine article is inspired; I mean God-breathed. In 2 Peter 1:21, we're told, "Prophecy never came by the will of man, but holy men of God spoke as they were moved by the Holy Spirit." The Holy Spirit used men to write the Scriptures. He used their personalities, their writing or speaking styles, and their vocabulary to convey the information God wanted to give to mankind. What we have here is worthy of our full attention. Through this message from God, we can find everything we need to fulfill the callings and positions He has given us. This means we are getting direction on leadership from God through Scripture. I don't think it's an overstatement to say this is the best source of instruction on leadership we have available.

Second, there is blessing for those who are obedient to the Word of God. One day, as Jesus was teaching, a woman cried out from the crowd, "Blessed is the womb that bore You, and the breasts which nursed You!" (Luke 11:27). Jesus' response was surprising: "More than that, blessed are those who hear the word of God and keep it!" Consider how blessed Mary was, being able to raise the Messiah. She truly was blessed among women, yet Jesus said that you are more blessed if you hear God's Word and you do it—you are literally living under a blessing! James also referred to this blessing: "He who looks into the perfect law of liberty and continues in it, and is not a forgetful hearer but a doer of the work, this one will be blessed in what he does" (James 1:25). When you listen and yield to the Word of God, you place yourself and your leadership under the blessings of God.

Third, when we apply biblical leadership principles, we are operating in faith, which can bring God's power into our leadership. When we believe in God's Word and do what God says in the Scriptures, that is faith. Here is a definition of faith I have found useful: "Faith is believing what God has said—believing enough to do it." And when you do that, God works on your behalf. Jesus said in Matthew 17:20, "Assuredly, I say to you, if you have faith as a mustard seed, you will say to this mountain, 'Move from here to there,' and it will move; and nothing will be impossible for you." Faith itself is not what is strong. If you put your faith in the wrong thing, you won't get the results you need.

In 1980, a book was published with the title *Having Faith in Your*

Faith. But the problem with putting faith in our faith should be obvious. Our faith is only as strong as what we put it in. When we put our faith in God, our faith becomes incredibly strong. We can move mountains, even if our faith in God is the size of a mustard seed. The issue isn't how much faith you have, but rather, putting your faith in the right place. When we talk about biblical leadership, we need to recognize that our power comes from the God who created the universe and everything in it and gave us the pages of Scripture.

GOOD AND BAD LEADERS

Standing in the auto shop of another employer, I asked myself, *How did I get here?* While applying pinstriping to the side of a car, I made a mistake. This isn't as bad as it sounds because you can easily remove and properly install the striping at minimal cost. But I didn't know that the owner of the auto shop was watching me. He came out in full anger mode. This was not uncommon; throughout the shop, everyone focused hard on what they were doing lest they become the subject of the owner's outbursts. Loud enough for everyone to hear, he began cursing and berating my work.

I had been hired to expand the shop to include an auto upholstery department. While we were getting the upholstery part of the shop built out, I was to work with everyone else putting accessories on cars—radios, cruise controls, side molding, and, yes, pinstriping. I had committed to staying employed at the shop for a year and a half while the auto upholstery department became established. What a long year and a half that was as I learned how detrimental a bad business leader can be! The morale at the shop was horrible, the turnover rate of employees was out of control, and the efficiency and quality of the work suffered.

There are many places we could go in Scripture to look at both good and bad leaders. However, some leaders are both good and bad.

Such is the case of one of the early kings of Judah, a king by the name of Asa. He starts out as a great leader, and over time, his leadership deteriorates. We will look at King Asa to learn some biblical lessons on both good and bad leadership.

LESSONS FROM KING ASA

The reign of King Asa was just a few generations after the reigns of King David and King Solomon. The kingdom of Israel had been divided into two regions—the kingdom of Israel and the kingdom of Judah. Jerusalem was the capital of Judah, and Samaria was the capital of Israel. In this divided nation, Asa sat on the throne of David in Judah.

We see the life of Asa broken up into five different stages, with the most tragic and greatest lesson coming in the last stage of King Asa's life. Here are the five stages:

- the new king
- the first leadership test
- a warning and positive response
- the second leadership test
- a final visit from a prophet

The people of Judah and Israel were living in a dark time, when idolatry was commonly accepted and widespread. They were supposed to worship God from Mount Moriah, where the temple was built. Instead, they worshipped idols on every high place, which means they would go to the tops of the hills and worship their false gods—including the gods of the Canaanites who had previously lived in that land. This had been an ongoing problem—in fact, the people had turned to foreign gods shortly after being delivered from slavery in Egypt. The time of the judges (before the kings) was also full of idolatry, with heroes like Gideon becoming involved. Idolatry was pervasive throughout Judah and Israel during the time Asa was king over Judah.

THE NEW KING

> Abijah rested with his fathers, and they buried him in the City of David. Then Asa his son reigned in his place. In his days the land was quiet for ten years. Asa did what was good and right in the eyes of the LORD his God (2 Chronicles 14:1-2).

We're told that because of Asa's good leadership, the land was at peace for ten years. Asa became one of the good kings—the first in a few generations.

Here we find our first leadership lesson:

1. Good leadership not only points the way, but also leads the way by example.

Asa led by example: He "did what was good and right in the eyes of the LORD his God."

When we lead, we're not just telling people what to do. We're setting an example and saying, "Follow me." Like Paul said, "Imitate me, just as I also imitate Christ" (1 Corinthians 11:1); he was leading the way in his relationship with God.

Back in 1985, when Skip Heitzig of Calvary Church in Albuquerque sent me to plant a church in Tucson, he shared two principles that were very important for me to know as a young pastor. First, he said, "Every time you get behind the pulpit, make sure things are right between you and God. Pause momentarily and make sure there's nothing you need to repent from so you can be a clean, pure vessel for God to use."

The second principle was this: "You won't bring people closer to

Christ than you are. Some of them may surpass you, but the majority of people won't get any closer to Jesus than you get."

That's great advice. May each one of us take these principles to heart. May we lead the way in our walk with Christ—in knowing the Word of God and in living in a close relationship with God.

Paul said to Timothy, who was a young pastor, "Let no one despise your youth, but *be an example* to the believers in word, in conduct, in love, in spirit, in faith, in purity" (1 Timothy 4:12).

Peter encourages us to be examples in our lives as well. "Shepherd the flock of God which is among you, serving as overseers, not by compulsion but willingly, not for dishonest gain but eagerly; nor as being lords over those entrusted to you, *but being examples* to the flock; and when the Chief Shepherd appears, you will receive the crown of glory that does not fade away" (1 Peter 5:2-4).

Leading by example meant removing the false gods, according to 2 Chronicles 14:3-4. Asa commanded the people of Judah to serve the Lord God of their fathers and tore down the altars and high places where they worshipped these false gods.

Here we find another leadership lesson:

2. Good leaders place a strong emphasis on doing what is right.

> To do righteousness and justice is more acceptable to the
> LORD than sacrifice (Proverbs 21:3).

Wherever you are leading, look at the culture in context to see what is harmful and ungodly, and be willing to confront it. Be strong enough to make corrections and remove what is wrong as you lead the people under you toward what is right. As a result of doing what was right, King Asa was given ten years of peace, and he used that time to build a large army and fortify the cities in Judah for protection from their enemies.

Then the first test arrived.

THE FIRST LEADERSHIP TEST

A king by the name of Zerah came out of Ethiopia (Africa) with a large army to do battle against Asa and Judah. Asa went out and set his troops in battle array. As he compared the size of his troops with Zerah's massive army, he realized, "I'm in trouble!" At that point, from a human perspective, Asa had two options. He could have retreated, or he could have gathered his generals and said, "Let's work out a strategy—let's figure out how we're going to defeat this larger army."

But that's not what he did. Instead, he called out to the Lord and relied on Him.

> Asa cried out to the LORD his God, and said, "LORD, it is nothing for You to help, whether with many or with those who have no power; help us, O LORD our God, for we rest on You, and in Your name we go against this multitude. O LORD, You are our God; do not let man prevail against You!" (2 Chronicles 14:11).

What a great prayer! Asa realized he was not alone, so he called out to God for help.

Here we find another leadership lesson:

3. Godly leaders lead by faith, placing their trust and hope in the Lord when there is a need.

This is a powerful leadership principle. Paul said in Romans 1:16-17:

> I am not ashamed of the gospel of Christ, for it is the power of God to salvation for everyone who believes, for the Jew first and also for the Greek. For in it the righteousness of God is revealed from faith to faith; as it is written, "The just shall live by faith."

That's what King Asa did. He put his faith in God, and God actively intervened, allowing Asa to defeat a larger army. "The LORD struck the Ethiopians before Asa and Judah, and the Ethiopians fled" (2 Chronicles 14:12).

Psalm 34:10 says, "The young lions lack and suffer hunger; but those who seek the LORD shall not lack any good thing." This happened with Asa, and God gave him the victory.

A WARNING AND POSITIVE RESPONSE

We now look at the next part of King Asa's life, during which God sends a prophet to encourage and warn him:

> Now the Spirit of God came upon Azariah the son of Oded. And he went out to meet Asa, and said to him: "Hear me, Asa, and all Judah and Benjamin. The LORD is with you while you are with Him. If you seek Him, He will be found by you; but if you forsake Him, He will forsake you...But you, be strong and do not let your hands be weak, for your work shall be rewarded!" (2 Chronicles 15:1-2, 7).

We're told that when Asa heard these words, he grew in his courage and removed more idols and restored the altar of the Lord. You might think, *Didn't they already do that?* But that was ten years previous, and a lot had changed. During the ten years after the idols had been cleared out, people slowly began to erect and worship idols again in the high places.

So when Asa heard these words from Oded the prophet, he took courage and removed the abominable idols from all the land of Judah and Benjamin, and from the cities that he had taken in the mountains of Ephraim during his fight against Zerah. He then restored the altar of the Lord because it had been broken down. Again, this was good on Asa's part. God had encouraged him, and he had stepped forward as a godly leader.

Second Chronicles 15:19 tells us, "There was no war until the thirty-fifth year of the reign of Asa." The first ten years were quiet. In the tenth year, he called upon God and fought a larger army, then there was peace for another 25 years. Asa had a good run up until this point!

Azariah's words in 2 Chronicles 15:2 remind me of James 4:8: "Draw near to God and He will draw near to you." If you feel far from God today, then draw near to Him. But do you know what the rest of the verse says? "Cleanse your hands, you sinners; and purify your hearts, you double-minded."

Here we find another leadership lesson:

4. Maintain a right relationship with God.

Our faithfulness ensures that God will fight for us when we are in need. If you're currently living away from God, you can call out to Him, and He will respond. God has said, "I will never leave you nor forsake you" (Hebrews 13:5). If you are distant from Him, now is the time to make things right.

Make a decision to repent and live your life God's way. To repent means to change our mind about sin and turn away from it. What peace is found in a right relationship with God! It's always much better to have a right relationship with God and to stay close to Him. Then you can have confidence that when you call upon Him in the middle of a struggle, He will be on your side.

This brings us to the fourth part of Asa's life.

THE SECOND LEADERSHIP TEST

After Asa's battle with the larger army from Ethiopia, there was peace in the land for 25 years. Then another conflict arose.

> In the thirty-sixth year of the reign of Asa, Baasha king of Israel came up against Judah and built Ramah, that he might let none go out or come in to Asa king of Judah (2 Chronicles 16:1).

Remember that Israel was a divided kingdom. King Asa ruled over the southern kingdom of Judah, and King Baasha ruled over the northern kingdom of Israel. The temple was in Jerusalem, which was in Judah. The law required the people to travel to Jerusalem for the feasts, but Baasha wanted them to stay in Israel. So Baasha built a fortified city, Ramah, between Israel and Judah, to prevent his people from going into Judah. This was a problem for Asa because God's people in Israel could not worship Him in Jerusalem, as God desired.

What did Asa do?

> Asa brought silver and gold from the treasuries of the house of the LORD and of the king's house, and sent to Ben-Hadad king of Syria, who dwelt in Damascus, saying, "Let there be a treaty between you and me, as there was between my father and your father. See, I have sent you silver and gold; come, break your treaty with Baasha king of Israel, so that he will withdraw from me" (2 Chronicles 16:2-3).

King Asa followed his father's example in making a treaty with Ben-Hadad, king of Syria, to overcome this problem, and he took money from the house of the Lord to do it. Ben-Hadad agreed with Asa's request and sent armies against the cities of Israel, which caused the people of Israel to cease their building of Ramah.

> Ben-Hadad heeded King Asa, and sent the captains of his armies against the cities of Israel. They attacked Ijon, Dan, Abel Maim, and all the storage cities of Naphtali.

> Now it happened, when Baasha heard it, that he stopped building Ramah and ceased his work. Then King Asa took all Judah, and they carried away the stones and timber of Ramah, which Baasha had used for building; and with them he built Geba and Mizpah (2 Chronicles 16:4-6).

It appears that Asa was successful. We could say again, "Good job, Asa!" However, a successful outcome does not determine the rightness of an act. There are many ways to be successful, but how many of them are God's way? Asa was a seasoned king; he knew how things were done in the world. When he was a young king, he recognized his insufficiency and called out on God. The danger of gaining more experience is that we tend to lean more on our knowledge and less on God, which is what happened to Asa.

This leads to another leadership lesson:

5. Success does not always mean you have done what is right and pleasing to God.

This is a mistake we as leaders are prone to make. Things are going great; everything is fantastic. In time, we begin to do things the way the world does. We stop seeking God or following His ways. In using worldly methods, we fail to trust God. Instead, we trust in silver and gold and the strength of men.

It's so easy for us to rely on our knowledge and what we've learned over the years instead of relying on God. In our prayer life, we need to bring everything before the Lord, even when we feel that we have what it takes to get the job done. Asa had access to the money in the treasury, and he had a relationship with Ben-Hadad to negotiate a treaty. He had what he needed to achieve a desired outcome, but he didn't seek God.

This brings us to the final, sad part of Asa's life.

A FINAL VISIT FROM A PROPHET

Again, it certainly looks like Asa was successful. But as we read on, we see that there's a problem.

> At that time Hanani the seer came to Asa king of Judah, and said to him: "Because you have relied on the king of Syria, and have not relied on the LORD your God, therefore the army of the king of Syria has escaped from your hand. Were the Ethiopians and the Lubim not a huge army with very many chariots and horsemen? Yet, because you relied on the LORD, He delivered them into your hand" (2 Chronicles 16:7-8).

When Asa first became king, he was young and served God for ten years. At his first test, he called out to God and God delivered him, and the land had peace for 25 years. Then at his second test, 35 years into his career as king, Asa feels like a veteran king. He's no longer young, and he knows how things are done. So he hires a mercenary army, as he had seen his father do. His thinking seemed rational: *Why send your people out into battle when you can hire mercenaries to go out and do battle for you?* But the army of the king of Syria (who later became a bigger enemy) escaped from King Asa. The consequence of Asa not trusting God was having wars in the future. Hanani reminded Asa of how God had delivered him from a previous battle against the huge army of the Ethiopians and the Lubim.

Hanani then speaks one of the great promises we find in the Scriptures, which is an excellent leadership lesson: "The eyes of the LORD run to and fro throughout the whole earth, to show Himself strong on behalf of those whose heart is loyal to Him" (2 Chronicles 16:9).

That brings us to our next lesson:

6. God will show Himself strong to those who are loyal to Him, trusting in Him rather than anything or anyone else.

God is looking for people who are loyal to Him. Are we trusting and relying on God, or are we placing our trust in ourselves or someone or something else? Are we figuring out the solutions to problems on our own, and going to God only when a problem is beyond our ability to handle? Or will we always call upon the Lord, having a loyal heart toward Him?

The first time I heard someone talk about 2 Chronicles 16:9, it was quoted out of context, which is not uncommon. I was told that if I could get rid of sin, God would show Himself strong toward me. Yes, we need to battle against sin, walk in God's grace, and find victory over strongholds. However, that is not the point of the passage, based on the context. Asa was loyal to God in the first battle, when he faced a larger army and called out to God for help. But in the second battle, he lacked loyalty toward God. He did not trust the Lord in the middle of a crisis. Instead, he trusted his business sense and a foreign army to deliver him and his people.

Now the story turns sad for our hero. The seer goes on to say,

> "In this you have done foolishly; therefore from now on you shall have wars." Then Asa was angry with the seer, and put him in prison, for he was enraged at him because of this. And Asa oppressed some of the people at that time (2 Chronicles 16:9-10).

Asa became enraged with the seer and put him in prison. Then he oppressed some of the people. Because of Asa's failures as a leader, people suffered under his leadership.

This brings us to another leadership principle:

7. Good leaders remain vigilant.

Just because you start well doesn't mean that you will end well. We must remain vigilant throughout our lives. How many people in the Bible started out good and ended bad? There are so many, and they are examples and warnings for us. We want to be vigilant in our faith so that in the end, we can hear those words: "Well done, good and faithful servant" (Matthew 25:23).

Read what Proverbs says about biblical leadership:

> When the righteous are in authority, the people rejoice; but when a wicked man rules, the people groan (Proverbs 29:2).

Because Asa was not being led by the Lord, he was oppressing the people, and they were groaning. Our decisions to rely on ourselves instead of God have long-term consequences and affect more people than we can imagine.

The end of Asa's life came in the forty-first year of his reign:

> In the thirty-ninth year of his reign, Asa became diseased in his feet, and his malady was severe; yet in his disease he did not seek the LORD, but the physicians. So Asa rested with his fathers; he died in the forty-first year of his reign (2 Chronicles 16:12-13).

DON'T DOUBLE DOWN ON SIN

What a tragedy that Asa doubled down on not seeking God. How sad that he made a mistake and then, when he was confronted with it, refused to repent. Asa could have responded another way. He could have said, "I have sinned against God," returned his loyalty to the Lord, and made things right with Him.

Instead, he hardened his heart. He put the prophet in prison, oppressed some of the people, and would not seek God even with a severe malady. There is nothing wrong with seeking physicians when we are sick, for God often uses physicians to heal us. But Asa refused to seek God at all. Though he had previously called upon God when he was young, 39 years later he would not even seek God for his healing, but instead he sought the knowledge of man.

When it comes to healing, James 5:14-15 says we're to "call for the elders of the church, and let them pray over him." We can pray that God will do a miraculous work of healing. There are two books that document miracles in our day: *Miracles Today* by Craig Keener, and *The Case for Miracles* by Lee Strobel. Just because we don't hear a lot about miracles doesn't mean God isn't doing them. But we are to pray and seek God in every matter, including sickness, and wait to see how He responds. To do this is to trust God in a much greater way than we trust physicians. And ultimate healing is granted when a faithful believer is taken to heaven.

THE BLESSING OF SEEKING GOD

Asa, who previously sought God and brought blessings to his people, died as a king who no longer trusted in God. His self-reliance resulted in defeat, misery, and the oppression of his people. It's so important for a leader to start well, but we must remain vigilant and continue seeking God in every area and season of our life so that we will finish well as leaders. This will bring huge blessings to us and to those we lead. Remember 2 Chronicles 15:7: "Be strong and do not let your hands be weak, for your work shall be rewarded!"

Among the many leadership lessons we gain from the life of King Asa, let's remember this:

> Remain loyal to the living God; put Him first in everything in your life—the good, the bad, and the ugly. This is so important to God, as He is on a search to show Himself strong to those whose hearts are loyal to Him.

CHAPTER 2

WHAT IS A GREAT LEADER?

Skip Heitzig

One Sunday morning during the height of the Civil War, President Abraham Lincoln walked from the White House to the National Presbyterian Church in Washington, DC. Distress and discouragement guided his steps as the reality of the war and the casualties on both sides weighed on him. He needed encouragement and guidance from God, so he and his aide sat in on an afternoon service. Afterward, President Lincoln's aide asked him if he had liked the sermon. The president considered his response, and finally replied that the sermon was well prepared and logical. He could follow the pastor's thinking from point to point. Overall, the sermon was delivered well.

His aide said, "So you thought it was a good sermon."

Lincoln replied, "No, I think he failed. He did not ask us to do something great."[1]

Unquestionably, Lincoln was a great leader, but he believed that other leaders (pastors included) should call people to not just do something good, but do something great. You've probably heard the old evangelical adage that says, "God loves you and has a wonderful plan for your life." Both aspects of that adage are true. He does love you, and He does have a great purpose for you to fulfill. God has called each of us to something great, leaders most of all. Luke 12:48 confirms this: "For everyone to whom much is given, from him much will be required; and to whom much has been committed, of him they will ask the more." The two most significant days in your life are the day you were born and the day you discover what you were born for. That second day is when you sense God's call for you to fulfill some great calling.

CONSIDERING DAVID'S CALL

David was born into a family of shepherds. The day of his birth was otherwise uneventful. As the youngest of eight sons, his early life was spent in the rigors of tending to his father's animals. But one day, a day recorded in 1 Samuel 16, David discovered what he was born for—to be the king of Israel. Though his road to leadership was a long journey, David's reign would become the gold standard for all of Israel's future kings.

As is the case with many leaders, despite God's big plans for David, his leadership qualities weren't recognized immediately. He was considered a loser—insignificant in the eyes of his own family. When his dad, Jesse, was instructed by the prophet Samuel to line up all his sons for a prospective roll call, he didn't think David was important enough to be included! But in God's time, David took the throne of Israel as shepherd-king and eventually became the ancestor of the Good Shepherd, the Messiah Himself. The big takeaway from David's life is that through faith and guidance, leaders can emerge and develop from loser status to leader status.

Don't be surprised if those called to leadership fail initially. Nobody but Christ is perfect, and modest means make for great leaders. Abraham Lincoln failed in politics and business ten times before he became president—he lost bids for Congress, the Senate, and lesser political offices. In 1856, his party rejected him for vice president.[2] Yet no one remembers him as a failure; they only remember his greatness. Four years later, he was elected to the highest office in the United States, and history attests to his status as one of America's greatest leaders.

Just as Lincoln was born to lead the United States during the most difficult season of its existence, and just as David was born to lead Israel after the dismal reign of its first king, Saul, you were born with your own call to lead. It's what God made you for. As Christian leaders, we belong to the greatest outfit in the world—the church—the only institution that Jesus said He would build.

If the church were a secular corporation, I suppose it could be considered "the greatest company" on earth. For one thing, *we have a product that works universally*. You can take it to any culture, and when rightly proclaimed, the gospel of Jesus Christ will change lives. Furthermore, *we have offices worldwide*—on every continent and in every language group, the church of Christ is represented in some fashion. Then *we have a benefits package* that includes forgiveness for our past sins, peace that surpasses understanding, and purpose for living. Finally, *we have a retirement package* that is out of this world: Heaven awaits us after our work is finished here. We're in a no-lose situation, and it's in that light that we're called to great things that the Lord has prepared in advance for us to do (Ephesians 2:10). But nothing worthwhile comes easily. Problems abound, and David's life was no exception.

In 1 Samuel 16, there was a leadership vacancy. Israel's first king, Saul, though still on the throne, had gotten a "no confidence vote" from God Himself (1 Samuel 13:14; 15:23; 16:1). The nation, devoid of real direction, was adrift like a rudderless ship. In the words of Charles Dickens, "It was the best of times, it was the worst of times."[3]

Most of us can relate to that on some level when it comes to leadership. When I moved from Southern California to Albuquerque to start a church, the change was both difficult and delightful. On one hand, it was the worst of times. I didn't know a soul in New Mexico. I left my family, friends, occupational network, and the daily surf sessions at the ocean. I had no money and my Datsun pickup truck (the brand no longer exists!) needed a quart of oil every 100 miles. And if all that wasn't enough, I now lived in a town whose name I couldn't even spell.

But those were also the best of times. I was following God's call for my life. I was newly married, and nothing beat hunkering down and praying with my wife about what God might want—trusting in Him for the next step, and then watching it happen. It's amazing to be able to step back and see the evidence of God' s calling upon one's life. It's a big risk, but it can also come with a big reward. The will of God can put us in strange places among unfamiliar people, often without any idea of what comes next. Despite all of that, God provides and prevails. He moves us according to His will and purpose. And His purpose is our highest calling.

From David's initial calling in 1 Samuel 16, we can glean four affirmations about godly leadership, and to help you remember, I've made them all rhyme: leadership is a necessity, it defies expectancy, it accompanies ability, and it rouses the enemy. Keep these truths in mind as you meditate on God's Word, pray for the Holy Spirit's guidance, and use your position as a leader to inspire others to do something great.

LEADERSHIP IS A NECESSITY

Did you know God is actively on the lookout for faithful leaders? "The eyes of the Lord run to and fro throughout the whole earth, to show Himself strong on behalf of those whose heart is loyal to Him" (2 Chronicles 16:9). God is looking for leaders who are committed to Him. He always has been. He seeks hearts that are devoted, that listen to Him, and that will pass on that commitment to others. Saul, at some point in his life, quit listening to God. He became paranoid, jealous, and reactive—everything a leader should *not* be—and this made him a dangerous person to have ruling a nation. He didn't lead people; he drove them. He was in a position of leadership, and though God was trying to work through him, the king refused to listen. That's a risky spot for any leader. When we start thinking we can do whatever we want because people are still showing up, or because we have a strong bottom line (and that must mean God is still using us), we have quit listening to God. Saul had done exactly this, and Samuel wasn't happy about it.

The prophet was mourning the failed king, and he must have been mourning for a while because 1 Samuel 16 opens with the Lord asking Samuel, "How long will you mourn for Saul…?" God announced to the prophet that He had rejected this first king, but the prophet was still brokenhearted. And rightfully so. Failed leadership is always a disappointment. Fallen heroes bring disillusionment to many and poison the well for aspiring ones. After confronting Saul, Samuel didn't see the failed monarch again this side of Sheol. But Samuel was deeply saddened nonetheless (1 Samuel 15:35). The Hebrew word translated "mourn" means to grieve as one would grieve for the dead. Saul had become dead to Samuel because he had hardened his heart to God. But there's a time to mourn and there's a time to move on (Ecclesiastes 3:2-8), and it was time for Samuel, under the direction of the Holy Spirit, to identify new leadership. He didn't need to lament the past, but rather, to learn from it and seek God's will for the future. God was already preparing the next leader and said, "I have provided Myself a king among [Jesse's] sons" (1 Samuel 16:1).

The Lord basically told Samuel this whole ordeal was His doing. He was responding sovereignly to Saul's failure. And He wasn't without a plan. He would do the heavy lifting to choose a new leader and close the chapter on the old one; Samuel was just the vessel—the messenger. As leaders, we would do well to remember this. If you are sifting through the wreckage left in the wake of failed leadership, remember that God is the primary leader. He saw this crisis coming and He has a vested interest in keeping His work going. Of course, we're part of it; we have a role to play, but keeping God's glory as our goal puts us in a winning position.

The failure or transiency of leadership doesn't upend God's plan; it only upsets God's people. Samuel mourned Saul's failure, just as we mourn every time a servant in ministry fails or passes on to heaven. But that mourning is rooted in our limited human perspective. God's perspective is much bigger, and His plan is much more durable. It's up to us to get past our mourning and discover what that plan is.

Vacancies in leadership happen for myriad reasons. Kings don't reign forever. Presidents don't hold office forever. Pastors and CEOs pass away. God's workmen may die, but God's work lives on. We often mistake new beginnings for the end. At a glance, a sunset and a sunrise are nearly indistinguishable. But God knows the difference.

When King Uzziah died, Judah's citizens were scared and confused. Even Isaiah the prophet was a bit shaken. The vacant throne of this good king could only mean disaster! But God was neither surprised nor anxious, and He assured Isaiah of His sovereign control through a vision. "It was in the year King Uzziah died that I saw the Lord. He was sitting on a lofty throne, and the train of his robe filled the Temple" (Isaiah 6:1 NLT). The message was clear: The most important Leader is still leading, and He has a plan. There's more than one workman, and when one leaves his position of leadership, another is called to take his place. God is ever and always forward-thinking. The past gives way to the future, from generation to generation. Great leaders will neither enshrine the past nor abandon it altogether. They learn from it and build on it, using it to further God's work in the place and position to which they've been called.

Warren Wiersbe said, "Over the years, I've seen churches and parachurch ministries flounder and almost destroy themselves in the futile attempt to embalm the past and escape the future. Their theme song was, 'As it was in the beginning, so shall it ever be, world without end.'"[4] Death is inevitable. Leaders move on. Change is constant. All pastors are interim pastors, and all leadership is provisional. But God is still on the throne. Just like Samuel, we need to heed the nudge of God when it's time to move on.

LEADERSHIP OFTEN DEFIES EXPECTANCY

Oftentimes, leaders aren't recognized at first, particularly leaders called by God, and David was no exception. Why? Well, God often calls leaders who don't meet our human expectations. We have ideas of what makes a strong leader, and most of these ideas are based on physical, outward appearance. Our concepts may include stature, tone of voice, confident mannerisms, and even bodily beauty. But a theme runs throughout the Bible: God's leaders are often overlooked at first. God picked Isaac over Ishmael and Jacob over Esau. Joseph, the youngest and most despised by his brothers, was the one God chose to elevate to a position of prominence so he could help his people during a time of famine.

And this theme continues into the New Testament. Jesus Christ was not brought up in Athens or Rome or even Jerusalem; He was raised in the backwater village of Nazareth. No one famous had come from this obscure hamlet. It was a nothing-town, just a stop on the way to someplace else. Nathanael asked if anything good could come out of Nazareth (John 1:46). It seems as soon as we ask if anything good could come out of a place or a person, God says, "I'm glad you asked. Watch this." That's God's method. Which leads me to what has become a life verse of Scripture for me.

First Corinthians 1:26-27 says, "You see your calling, brethren, that not many wise according to the flesh, not many mighty, not many noble, are called. But God has chosen the foolish things of the world to put to shame the wise, and God has chosen the weak things of the world to put to shame the things which are mighty." This passage has been a guiding light in my heart. I love that God deliberately chooses the oft-overlooked for greatness and leadership. His ways are so unlike our ways. His choices are often utterly counter to human choices. Why does He do it? Simple: He gets more glory that way. Paul explains it like this: "[So] that no flesh should glory in His presence" (1 Corinthians 1:29). When God uses weak, timid, overlooked, unimpressive, or marginalized people to do something great, everyone can see that a mighty God is at work.

It's like a surgical operation. When a doctor performs surgery in a modern hospital filled with the latest medical technology, computerized scalpels, and ample assistants, good results are par for the course. But when the same doctor has rudimentary tools (say, a pocketknife and flashlight) and performs the operation in a jungle hut in central Africa, everyone takes notice. That doctor's genius is rightfully highlighted. The cruder the instruments to which the physician is confined, the more glory and notability that physician will receive. This is why great leaders identify their God-given talents and their God-empowered gifts and rely *only* on God's power, not their own. Anything else can, and often does, end in disaster.

The standards by which most people measure leadership qualities are natural and external. It happened in David's case. God's standards weren't even considered by the humans involved. Samuel's impulse was to judge on appearance. David's brother Eliab looked regal like Saul. He had great physical prowess. He looked the part. So naturally, Samuel thought he was the guy. But God said he was wrong (1 Samuel 16:6-7).

Jesse's standard was age. Working from the well-established law of primogeniture, he paraded before the prophet all his sons from the eldest on down, except for one—the youngest. Jesse even admitted that was his reason. "There remains yet the youngest, and there he is, keeping the sheep" (verse 11). Age was most important to Jesse. But God said he was wrong (verse 10). Samuel and Jesse were so busy looking at the packaging that they didn't consider the contents. God, on the other hand, is all about the contents, not the packaging.

David's anointing for kingship took everybody by surprise—even David. It was not the life he expected nor desired. He was raised for the pasture. He didn't think he would ever live in a palace until it happened. But that was the best possible outcome for the struggling nation of Israel. Unlike Saul, who drove his people, David was a shepherd. You can't drive sheep. They must be led. They can't be ruled or forced into obedience, but rather, must be escorted with gentle guidance. So, in David, Israel was getting the shepherd and leader it needed. No humans saw it at first, but God did.

There is another layer that mustn't be overlooked. Notice that in selecting the next leader of Israel, God went to the youngest. He reached into the upcoming generation. There's an important lesson there. Any organization left to itself will naturally grow older and turn inward. What was young and innovative a few years ago can sometimes become stagnant and passé. That's not to say that our vision should focus only on young people, but it shouldn't focus solely on old people either. It should focus on all God's people. God knew this and accomplished it through David. God chose a young man who was committed to God's established Word, but forward-thinking in his faith and relationship to Him. He had the energy and strength of youth mixed with a loyal heart toward God. Would he make mistakes? He would make plenty of them, but none were insurmountable. I think that's a good model.

Many of us are familiar with 1 Samuel 13:14: "The Lord has sought for Himself a man after His own heart." A better translation of "after His own heart" is "in harmony with Him." In David, God chose a man whose heart was in harmony with His heart. A great leader is someone who has a great heart for a great God. That means what is important to God is important to the one in harmony with Him. Conversely, what burdens God burdens the one in harmony with Him. Robert Townsend said, "A leader is a person who has a magnet in his heart and a compass in his head."[5] In other words, he directs his thinking where his heart is fixed. God is all about the heart.

What's in your heart? The size of your organization and the size of your budget are irrelevant if your heart isn't properly directed. Are you a man or a woman in harmony with God's heart? Consider this before you answer. Jeremiah 17:9 says, "The heart is deceitful above all things...who can know it?" Only God really can. Maybe this is why David prayed, "Search me, O God, and know my heart; try me, and know my anxieties" (Psalm 139:23). That's a good prayer to pray often as a leader. Ask God to help you see what's happening inside you. God knows your heart. And He can bring people into your life who will tell you the truth if you let them. So, let them. True accountability means having people around who will tell you the truth when you need to hear it.

LEADERSHIP IS ACCOMPANIED BY ABILITY

Imagine the pandemonium that must've occurred in the little town of Bethlehem that day. To start, Samuel was wary of making the trip because he knew that if Saul found out, the king would be suspicious about his visit (1 Samuel 16:2). The citizens of Bethlehem were nervous when the prophet came—for the same reason (verse 4). Then Jesse and his boys were given the royal inspection by Samuel, only to be rejected (verses 6-10). And finally, David got pulled out of the pasture and brought before this solemn assembly. He noticed his brothers were moping around as he was presented to the prophet Samuel. Perhaps Samuel briefly tilted his head, listening for the still, small voice of God that had rejected all of David's brothers. With a tiny nod, Samuel acknowledged that voice and then, without warning, dumped a hornful of oil on David's head.

David, dripping oil, was probably dumbfounded, wondering what that was all about. According to Josephus,[6] the prophet leans in at this point and explains what's going on: "You're gonna be king, kid." What shocking news this must have been to David! As far as he was concerned, he didn't have the credentials to be king. But we're told "the Spirit of the Lord came upon David from that day forward" (verse 13). God was equipping him for the calling. The Holy Spirit would enable David to do the impossible—shepherd a nation. The adage is true: *God doesn't call those who are qualified. He qualifies those whom He calls.*

If you joined the army, the government wouldn't make you buy your own uniform, weapons, and ammo. If you become an airline pilot, the company wouldn't ask you to provide your own plane. If you get drafted onto a major league baseball team, you wouldn't have to raise funds for your uniforms, bats, and other equipment. So it is with God's kingdom. With the calling comes the anointing. With the anointing comes the gifting. With the gifting comes the enabling. If God has called you, it will be evident. Paul said to the Ephesian elders, "This is God's flock, of whom the Holy Spirit made you overseers" (see Acts 20:28).

This fact should never be far from the hearts and minds of those whom God calls to lead His flock. Do not touch the ministry unless the Holy Spirit has guided you to it. And if the calling of leadership has truly been granted, it will be evident because you'll be gifted to lead and to feed. God will provide all that's needed for you to do the task. But supernatural ability does not negate human responsibility. Leaders still need to study, work, plan, outline, meet, strategize, problem-solve, and pray. Think of it as a divine partnership, a cooperation between heaven and earth. "We are co-workers in God's service," wrote the apostle Paul (1 Corinthians 3:9 NIV). He will certainly do His part, and we must do ours!

Let me speak candidly to those leaders who are also pastors: Don't enter or stay in ministry expecting an easy time. As Charles Haddon Spurgeon admonished his pastoral students, "If you plan to be lazy there are plenty of vocations in which you will not be wanted. But above all, you are not wanted in the Christian ministry. The man who finds the ministry an easy life will also find that it will bring a hard death."[7]

Paul cautioned Timothy to "be diligent to present yourself approved to God." He described the pastor as "a worker who does not need to be ashamed, rightly dividing the word of truth" (2 Timothy 2:15). Paul wrote this to a younger pastor, and it's great advice for any leader. Confidence is directly linked to preparation. Don't try to shortcut the long haul. The hard work pays great dividends in the end. If you're a pastor reading this, know that God's anointing will gift you with needed insight when you study the biblical text and give you the ability to effectively preach it. But if you believe that, you will take the time to really study it. Somebody worth listening to is somebody who has processed the text in the presence of the Holy Spirit. They have something to say.

LEADERSHIP WILL ROUSE THE ENEMY

Saul's jealousy and anger were eventually aimed at David. As God's anointed leader, David was now a high-value target. "A distressing spirit" troubled king Saul (1 Samuel 16:14) and he tried to exterminate the new competition (1 Samuel 18:9, 11; 19:10; 20:31). David became the most hunted "criminal" in Israel for almost a decade. Why? When God calls someone to step into leadership, a bull's-eye is painted on that individual. The new leader becomes the target of an old enemy. Anyone at the center of God's plan likewise becomes the center of Satan's ire, and Satan did everything he could to take David out.

I don't think many leaders realize the extent of the opposition they'll face going into God's work. Great leaders have great enemies that mount great opposition. The discouragement, the spiritual attacks, the frustration all burden God's leaders in ways they don't expect. Sadly, many can't carry the burden. Every month, about 1,500 ministers leave the ministry. Studies have shown that 50 percent of ministers and church leaders would quit the ministry, but they don't have any other skill set.[8]

Spiritual attack is an occupational hazard; the devil knows what's on the line—the souls of people in our congregations and communities, not to mention the spiritual growth of believers. That's why pastors, ministers, and ministry leaders are targeted. It comes with the territory. Did you really think that if you stepped into spiritual leadership, hell would give you a standing ovation? To be honest, a leader is like a tea bag; he's not worth much until he's been through some hot water!

If the burden of God's calling is starting to weigh you down, consider the young father who was excited to have a baby. When the child finally came, he hadn't anticipated the noise. He hadn't anticipated the demands, the constant feeding, and the dozen diapers a day he would have to change. Neither did his wife. And one day, he heard his wife, as she was changing a diaper, say, "Honey, I'm starting to forget what our baby's face looks like. I've been spending so much time at the wrong end."[9]

Maybe the wrong end of ministry has been getting all your attention. You've seen all the bad stuff. You live in the muck and mire day after day, month after month. Eventually, it takes its toll on you. The life of a leader can be discouraging. You start imagining life without all the dirty diapers. But look for the better "end" of it—the beautiful faces of souls impacted for God's glory.

IT'S ALL ABOUT THE HEART

Is there anything wrong with wanting to be a great leader? I ask that question honestly. At God's behest, Jeremiah asked his scribe, Baruch, "Do you seek great things for yourself? Do not seek them" (Jeremiah 45:5). Charles Spurgeon wanted to attend a prestigious college in England but missed his entrance appointment. Walking away discouraged, he recalled this verse in Jeremiah about not seeking greatness. Yet he went on to become one of the greatest preachers in history!

In some Christian circles, it's considered taboo to want to do great things for God because it could foster pride and countermand humility. So how do we step into greatness as leaders while staying humble? That's a fair question, but did you know that greatness and humility actually go hand in hand? Jesus explained it this way: "Whoever exalts himself will be humbled, and he who humbles himself will be exalted" (Matthew 23:12).

Remember President Lincoln's evaluation of the preacher: "He did not ask us to do something great." Don't be afraid to do big things! You believe in a big God, so why not go for it? But don't forget that it's all about the heart. Humility is the pathway to promotion. Take Jeremiah's example: Don't seek great things *for yourself*. Seek God. Seek His Word. Stay humble. Go low so God can unfold great plans for your life. As you stay teachable, approachable, correctable, and transparent in heart, God will promote you to a position where you can thrive and influence others. Great things lay ahead for those who stay close to God's heart and tethered to His Word.

A plane flying in California stopped in Sacramento for a layover. The pilot announced the layover would be 45 minutes long and asked the passengers to disembark for a 30-minute break. Everybody got off the plane except one blind man. This gentleman was flying with his seeing-eye dog. The pilot must have known the passenger because he went up to him and said, "Hey, James, we're all getting off. Would you like to stretch your legs?" James said, "No. I'm just going to stay aboard the plane, but my dog could use a walk."

The pilot decided he would do that for the man. When the pilot stepped off the plane with a seeing-eye dog and sunglasses on, the passengers in the lobby went berserk. Everybody started scrambling, looking for a different plane to catch.[10] Why was there such a reaction? They had no desire to trust their lives to a man who couldn't see to fly. And leaders who don't live by the Bible have no business flying God's plane with God's flock as passengers. Keep your heart pure and take your leadership cues from God's flight manual. If you focus yourself and those you lead on the greatness of God, you're sure to prosper.

CHAPTER 3

KEYS TO EFFECTIVE LEADERSHIP FROM NEHEMIAH

Gary Hamrick

Leadership styles vary. But every leadership style must contain some common criteria, and *courage* is essential. And in the Bible, one of the best examples of a courageous leader is Nehemiah.

The story of Nehemiah is recorded in the Old Testament book that bears his name. The year is circa 445 BC, and it is the twentieth year of the reign of the Persian king Artaxerxes.

Nehemiah's name, in Hebrew, means "God comforts." He is a Jew living among the Jewish exiles in Persia, which is modern-day Iran, and he serves in the palace of the king as a cupbearer. The role of the cupbearer was unlike what we sometimes imagine—that of a guinea pig who would sample the king's wine or food before the king consumed it to make certain it did not contain anything poisonous. In contrast, a cupbearer was a trusted, seasoned advisor to the king rather than simply an expendable member of the king's court who taste-tested everything for poison. The cupbearer was an honorable, reliable, influential member of the king's court, and he was carefully selected as a confidant of the king who would be absolutely trusted without reservation. This was Nehemiah.

How he got the role of a cupbearer—such a prestigious and honorable position—is unknown (aside from the fact that God had obviously promoted him to a position of influence). What is better understood is how he ended up as a Jew living in Persia, or what was previously Babylon. Nehemiah was born and raised there. He was living among the Jewish exiles who had been transplanted there several generations earlier when King Nebuchadnezzar of Babylon had besieged the city of Jerusalem beginning in 606 BC, conquering it by 586 BC, and deporting thousands of Jews to Babylon over the course of those 20 years.

The Babylonians were subsequently conquered by the Medes and the Persians. The Medo-Persian king Cyrus issued an edict, circa 538 BC, that any of the Jews who had been living there in captivity over the last 70 years under the Babylonian Empire were now free to return to their homeland of Israel. Some happily returned, but many decided to stay. Nehemiah's family was among those Jews who had chosen to remain in Persia.

Thus, not only was Nehemiah born in this Babylonian-Persian region, but he had also never been to Israel, the land of his Jewish forefathers. He hadn't personally seen the devastation that was the result of the Babylonian invasion of Jerusalem decades earlier. But in the opening chapter of Nehemiah, we read that Nehemiah learns about the dilapidated condition of Jerusalem from his brother and a few other men who had visited the city. They reported to Nehemiah not only the physical condition of the city itself, but also the declining moral and cultural climate of the Jewish people who had returned there under King Cyrus's edict. None of the news was good. And when Nehemiah heard this report, he was so heartbroken and burdened by it all that he requested, and was granted, permission from King Artaxerxes to travel to Jerusalem to lead the people in rebuilding the city walls.

THE CHARACTERISTICS OF EFFECTIVE LEADERSHIP

There are several commendable attributes Nehemiah displayed as a courageous leader that are worth emulating—attributes we will explore in the rest of this chapter.

1. A leader must be both tough and tender.

In Nehemiah chapter 1, we see Nehemiah weeping over the sad condition of Jerusalem and the Jewish people. But in the last chapter of the book, we see him beating up men and pulling their beards for their lack of moral character! (Nehemiah 13:25). One of the qualities I admire most about Nehemiah's leadership is that he was both tough and tender.

Jesus was the perfect example of such a balanced leader. He exemplified both toughness and tenderness. There were times when He revealed His tender side. He wept over Jerusalem (Matthew 23:37-39). He wept at Lazarus' tomb (John 11:35). And He wept at other unspecified times in Scripture (Hebrews 5:7).

But Jesus also showed a tough side. In John 2:13-22, near the beginning of His ministry, He braided a whip and drove out the moneychangers from the temple in Jerusalem. Three years later, near the end of His ministry, He again displayed His righteous indignation by driving out the moneychangers, as recorded in Matthew 21:12-17.

The key to effective leadership is to know which to exercise when.

There are times a leader needs to be tough, and there are times a leader needs to be tender, and one had better not confuse the two!

If you're tender at a time when you should be tough, people will be allowed to get away with things they shouldn't, and that will have devastating results in the long term. On the other hand, if you're tough when you should be tender, you're going to end up crushing some people along the way and leaving a trail of wounded souls.

If you're a parent, you understand this delicate dance. My wife, Terri, and I have three grown children—Tyler, Austin, and Lindsey. When they were young and still living at home, whenever we caught them misbehaving, they responded to our parenting in slightly different ways. All Tyler needed was a stern glance, and he would quickly conform. All Lindsey needed was a firm word, and she also would quickly conform. To do more would have crushed their young spirits. But our middle child, Austin, needed more—a stern glance or a firm word would not have been enough. Each child responded better to different types of leadership (parenting), and the key is to know which type to exercise when. (Side note: I am happy to report that all three children turned out wonderfully by the grace of God! All three have a strong relationship with Jesus, all three married Christian spouses, and all three serve on staff at our church, Cornerstone Chapel—all to the glory of God!)

So whether you're in a leadership role in a ministry, an organization, a business, or a family, sometimes you need to be tough, and sometimes you need to be tender. We see Nehemiah weeping in the first chapter of his book after he had heard about the devastating condition of the walls around Jerusalem: "When I heard these words… I sat down and wept, and mourned for many days; I was fasting and praying before the God of heaven" (Nehemiah 1:4).

Notice that when Nehemiah wept, his sorrow wasn't an emotional, knee-jerk reaction. He coupled it with prayer and fasting, which leads us to our second point:

2. A leader does not react to things out of emotion but out of devotion to God through prayer and fasting.

For a leader, there are decisions that must be made, and people who must be managed. There are time demands, deadlines, and schedules to plan. There are meetings to conduct, budgets to be met, and staff to be hired. All of this takes wisdom and discernment! And much of that can be gained through prayer and fasting.

In Matthew 17, Jesus took three of His disciples (Peter, James, and John) up on the Mount of Transfiguration, and He left the other nine down at the base of the mountain. The nine went on to have an encounter with a father whose son was suffering from demon possession. The disciples tried everything they could to deliver this boy, but to no avail. When Jesus descended from the mountain with Peter, James, and John, He was approached by the boy's father: "Lord, have mercy on my son, for he is an epileptic and suffers severely; for he often falls into the fire and often into the water. So I brought him to Your disciples, but they could not cure him" (Matthew 17:15-16).

Jesus did for the boy what His disciples could not. After Jesus had cast out the demon, He explained to His disciples, "This kind does not go out except by prayer and fasting" (verse 21).

Prayer and fasting are often-neglected disciplines that can be great tools for leaders who want to acquire the strength, power, discernment, and wisdom their jobs demand.

Oswald Chambers once said,

> We tend to use prayer as a last resort, but God wants it to be our first line of defense. We pray when there's nothing else we can do, but God wants us to pray before we do anything at all. Most of us would prefer, however, to spend our time doing something that will get immediate results. We don't want to wait for God to resolve matters in His good time because His idea of "good time" is seldom in sync with ours.[1]

Isaiah 58 is a great chapter on the importance of fasting. I encourage you to read it. There is a wonderful correlation between denying physical food and being more attuned to the things of the Spirit. The Puritans used to call fasting "soul fattening" because in the process of denying food to our stomachs, our souls become full!

In our story in Nehemiah, when the Jewish exiles returned to their homeland (or more accurately, *arrived* at their homeland for the first time, since most of them were born in Persia and had never seen Israel), they arrived to rubble! There were no fields ready to be harvested, no homes ready to be inhabited, and there was no temple ready to be occupied for worship. The walls of the city had been completely destroyed, and there was no way that the people could survive except by the grace of God. So when Nehemiah heard about all this, he wept, he fasted, prayed, and then he felt called by God to go to Jerusalem to lead the rebuilding project.

After getting the blessings and permission of King Artaxerxes, Nehemiah traveled roughly 1,000 miles from the Persian palace in Shushan to the city of Jerusalem, accompanied only by a military envoy. Notice what Nehemiah did when he made this journey: "I told no one what my God had put in my heart to do at Jerusalem" (Nehemiah 2:12). That brings us to the next key:

3. A leader keeps some things between himself or herself and God.

There are times when it's wise to ponder things between yourself and God. You don't want to act or react until you know exactly what God wants you to do. Learn to wait upon the Lord. Psalm 27:14 says: "Wait on the LORD; be of good courage, and He shall strengthen your heart; wait, I say, on the LORD!"

Look at the example of Mary, the mother of Jesus. When Mary was told by the angel Gabriel that she would conceive and give birth to the Messiah, Luke 2:19 says that Mary "kept all these things and pondered them in her heart." She didn't go around telling everyone what Gabriel said.

Can you imagine if that were to happen today? Most 15-year-old girls, if they were to be visited by an angel about a miraculous conception, would be trying to take selfies with Gabriel so they could post the news all over social media! The whole world would know about it in a nanosecond.

Not Mary. She was, in effect, saying, "I'm pondering this. I'm not going to talk about it, and I'm not going to broadcast this. I'm simply going to meditate on this. I'm going to pray through this. This is overwhelming."

Leaders need to understand that sometimes it's best to "pray it, don't say it." We need to internalize what God is telling us, not publicize it. We need to dwell on it, not tell it. Sometimes we just need to keep things between ourselves and God until the time is right to talk.

There would come a time when Nehemiah would talk, but only after he had inspected the city walls and gates.

> I went up in the night by the valley, and viewed the wall; then I turned back and entered by the Valley Gate, and so returned. And the officials did not know where I had gone or what I had done; I had not yet told the Jews, the priests, the nobles, the officials, or the others who did the work.
>
> Then I said to them, "You see the distress that we are in, how Jerusalem lies waste, and its gates are burned with fire. Come and let us build the wall of Jerusalem, that we may no longer be a reproach" (Nehemiah 2:15-17).

Nehemiah quietly examined the walls and the gates around the southern part of the city. He saw the disrepair and devastation. Then at the right time, Nehemiah told his fellow Jews why he was there and what he was doing, and he called upon them to get involved and help. He urged them to roll up their sleeves and get to work! And they responded with enthusiasm: "'Let us rise up and build.' Then they set their hands to this good work" (verse 18).

4. A leader inspires people to work, then leads by example.

When you look at the chronology of events and the history of what had transpired in this story, the Jews who had returned to Jerusalem before Nehemiah's arrival had never taken time to rebuild the city walls or establish themselves within the city of Jerusalem. They were living on the *outskirts* of the city. But they *had* rebuilt the altar of the Lord at the original site of the temple *inside* the city and were content to step over all the rubble every time they went from their homes to the temple area to worship the Lord. How tragic that they were so unmotivated to rebuild, and so willing to accept the ruinous condition of their city!

Nehemiah basically said to the people, "This isn't right. We don't have protection. Everything is in a state of disrepair. We must work and rebuild the walls."

In Nehemiah 4, when the rebuilding project was under way, the Jews came under attack from their neighbors to the north and the east. First came a war of words and intimidation from two leaders—Sanballat, the governor of Samaria, and Tobiah, a Persian official from Ammon, which is modern-day Jordan.

Nehemiah 4:1-3 tells us what took place:

> It so happened, when Sanballat heard that we were rebuilding the wall, that he was furious and very indignant, and mocked the Jews. And he spoke before his brethren and the army of Samaria, and said, "What are these feeble Jews doing? Will they fortify themselves? Will they offer sacrifices? Will they complete it in a day? Will they revive the stones from the heaps of rubbish—stones that are

> burned?" Now Tobiah the Ammonite was beside him, and he said, "Whatever they build, if even a fox goes up on it, he will break down their stone wall."

Well, aren't these guys a couple of comedians? They are laughing it up and mocking the Jews about their building project. But it's no laughing matter because behind the mocking is anger. Notice again in verse 1 that Sanballat "was furious and very indignant." He and Tobiah hated who the Jews were and what the Jews were doing. And the Jews understood their enemies' hatred. They realized that at any moment the war of words could escalate to a war of weapons. And that's exactly what happened.

> All of them conspired together to come and attack Jerusalem and create confusion...And our adversaries said, "They will neither know nor see anything, till we come into their midst and kill them and cause the work to cease."
>
> So it was, when the Jews who dwelt near them came, that they told us ten times, "From whatever place you turn, they will be upon us."
>
> Therefore I [Nehemiah] positioned men behind the lower parts of the wall, at the openings; and I set the people according to their families, with their swords, their spears, and their bows. And I looked, and arose and said to the nobles, to the leaders, and to the rest of the people, "Do not be afraid of them. Remember the Lord, great and awesome, and fight for your brethren, your sons, your daughters, your wives, and your houses" (verses 8, 11-14).

Whoa, whoa, wait a minute, Nehemiah! You sound like a Second Amendment freak with an NRA bumper sticker on your horse. You're arming your people with weapons? I thought Christians were supposed to turn the other cheek. What's up with the weapons?

Kidding aside...since when did *meekness* become *weakness*? Since when did *peaceful* become *passive*? There are some things worth defending, and chief among them is your family! Look at verse 14 again: "Remember the Lord, great and awesome, and fight for your brethren, your sons, your daughters, your wives, and your houses."

Nehemiah continued,

> So it was, from that time on, that half of my servants worked at construction, while the other half held the spears, the shields, the bows, and wore armor; and the leaders were behind all the house of Judah. Those who built on the wall, and those who carried burdens, loaded themselves so that with one hand they worked at construction, and with the other held a weapon. Every one of the builders had his sword girded at his side as he built. And the one who sounded the trumpet was beside me (verses 16-18).

Notice that Nehemiah was *not* advocating aggression or violence. He was advocating a strong defense and the need for the people to protect their families and homes.

5. A leader fights for what is right.

We are living in a dangerous time when the culture wants your family, and particularly your children. They're going after the next generation, and they have an intentional agenda.

In Loudoun County, Virginia, where I pastor, the school board passed Policy 8040, which allows children to identify as whatever gender they choose, and the policy requires fellow students and teachers to address those children by their preferred pronouns. The same policy prohibits schools or teachers from notifying parents of a child's gender pronoun preference. Even though parents must grant permission for their child to be given Tylenol at school, they are denied their parental rights when it comes to being notified about their child's gender dysphoria or pronoun preference.

The world wants to capture the hearts and minds of the next generation, and we must protect our families. We must, as Nehemiah said, work hard "with a weapon in one hand," figuratively speaking, as we work with the other hand. We've got to be on our guard. The enemy and the world want your children, your wife, your husband—all those who are closest to you. Which is why you need to fight for them.

In Nehemiah chapter 5, we read that under the leadership of Nehemiah, the rebuilding of the walls of Jerusalem was nearly done. But then difficulties and challenges arose from within the Jewish community that threatened the completion of the project.

The king of Persia had allowed the Jews to rebuild Jerusalem. He had even financially supported the project. But to recover his expenses, the king taxed the Jewish people living in Jerusalem because the region was part of the Persian Empire.

This created a great burden on the Jewish people living there because there was no infrastructure available to support them economically. It took time to rebuild the city and to rebuild their lives in a new land. Theirs was an agrarian culture, and it took time for them to plant and harvest fields, raise livestock, develop land, and produce income streams. They didn't have a lot of money, and many of them found it difficult to pay their taxes. So those who had financial means started taking advantage of those who *didn't* have such means, and they began to make all these unreasonable demands in exchange for paying the taxes of those who couldn't afford to do so.

If you couldn't pay your taxes, one of your fellow Jews who had the means to do so would pay your tax bill in exchange for your land, or worse, your children! That's right—land and children would be sold to the highest bidder. Imagine that! People were having to sell their own children into slavery so that their taxes could be paid to the government.

Nehemiah 5:5 says,

> Yet now our flesh is as the flesh of our brethren, our children as their children; and indeed we are forcing our sons and our daughters to be slaves, and some of our daughters have been brought into slavery. It is not in our power to redeem them, for other men have our lands and vineyards.

The Israelites were bemoaning their situation and complaining to Nehemiah. He responded with anger in verse 6: "I became very angry when I heard their outcry and these words."

And so Nehemiah intervened. He rebuked the nobles and the officials. He demanded that they return the lands and the children that they had extorted from their fellow Jews, and admonished them to serve and care for each other instead.

6. A leader deals with internal conflict.

Please don't avoid the hard stuff as a leader. Nobody likes conflict, or at least nobody *should* like conflict. But I have learned over 30-plus years of ministry that if I try to avoid conflict over the little things, the little things will inevitably become the big things, and the big things are more difficult to resolve. It's the little foxes that ruin the vineyard.

Some years ago, I had a staff member who was undermining me. He would say "little" things, "subtle" things, to other staff members or people in the congregation that expressed his disagreement with me or with the things that I taught. So I had to confront him. If I had dismissed his comments as inconsequential, I would have ended up with a bigger problem down the road.

Unfortunately, this staff person not only admitted to doing this, but he continued to undermine me after being warned, so I fired him. Sometimes we are afraid to do the hard thing because we're concerned about the potential fallout. I knew this guy had friends in the church who might leave with him. But we must trust the Lord with the outcome if we believe that we are doing what is right and necessary.

Nehemiah understood this. He knew he had to deal with *internal* conflict. And if that wasn't bad enough, according to Nehemiah chapter 6, he also had to deal with *external* conflict.

Nehemiah faced continual outside opposition from the "three stooges"—Sanballat, Tobiah, and Geshem. He said in verse 2 that "they thought to do me harm." These guys did everything they could to wear down Nehemiah with fear, intimidation, and harassment. They were unrelenting with their antagonism and opposition. Four times, they tried to get him off course. But a leader doesn't move off mission.

> Now it happened when Sanballat, Tobiah, Geshem the Arab, and the rest of our enemies heard that I had rebuilt the wall, and that there were no breaks left in it (though at that time I had not hung the doors in the gates), that Sanballat and Geshem sent to me, saying, "Come, let us meet together among the villages in the plain of Ono." But they thought to do me harm.
>
> So I sent messengers to them, saying, "I am doing a great work, so that I cannot come down. Why should the work cease while I leave it and go down to you?"
>
> But they sent me this message four times, and I answered them in the same manner (verses 1-4).

7. A leader stays focused despite criticism and opposition.

You will always have your critics. And if you let them, they can become a great distraction to what you're supposed to be doing.

Four times, they tried to get Nehemiah off point, and four times, he gave them the same reply: "I am doing a great work, so that I cannot come down. Why should the work cease while I leave it and go down to you?" (verse 3).

Somebody once told me, "Discount the high end and the low end of flattery and criticism." Who you really are is probably somewhere in the middle. Some people will think that you're the greatest teacher, or the greatest pastor, or the greatest CEO, or the greatest whatever, but it isn't true. But neither is the other extreme true, when people are highly critical. We are usually somewhere in the middle of high praise and low criticism. Don't let the flattery go to your head, and don't let the criticism go to your heart. Stay on mission!

From Nehemiah 8 we find the eighth point for a leader—especially one who is leading a church or ministry organization:

8. A leader prioritizes the Word of God.

> Now all the people gathered together as one man in the open square that was in front of the Water Gate; and they told Ezra the scribe to bring the Book of the Law of Moses, which the LORD had commanded Israel. So Ezra the priest brought the Law before the assembly of men and women and all who could hear with understanding on the first day of the seventh month. Then he read from it in the open square that was in front of the Water Gate from morning until midday, before the men and women and those who could understand; and the ears of all the people were attentive to the Book of the Law (Nehemiah 8:1-3).

There has been a neglect of God's Word in many churches today. Some churches are more concerned about social justice and hanging statement flags on their front doors than they are about equipping people with the Word of God. In contrast, Nehemiah 8 says the Jewish people gave great devotion to the Word of God and made it central to their lives. Verse 18 adds, "Also day by day, from the first day until the last day, [Ezra] read from the Book of the Law of God."

The Word of God was central to them. It was a priority. Isaiah tells us in Isaiah 40:8, "The grass withers, the flower fades, but the word of our God stands forever." Your Bible is God's love letter to you and to me, breathed by the Spirit of God, to reveal the person of God and the purposes of God. And we must not shortchange people from understanding the life-changing work of God's Word.

I've seen alcoholics and addicts get their lives sober and clean because they started reading the Bible. I've seen self-centered men become godly husbands and wonderful dads because they started reading the Word of God. I've seen insecure women become confident, godly women because they were reading the Word of God.

Psalm 19:7-8 says, "The law of the LORD is perfect, converting the soul; the testimony of the LORD is sure, making wise the simple; the statutes of the LORD are right, rejoicing the heart; the commandment of the LORD is pure, enlightening the eyes."

And that's exactly what happens in this story. Nehemiah 8:10 says, "Then he said to them, 'Go your way, eat the fat, drink the sweet, and send portions to those for whom nothing is prepared; for this day is holy to our Lord. Do not sorrow, for the joy of the LORD is your strength.'"

Our last point comes from Nehemiah 13:

9. A leader is responsible for maintaining a high moral standard for the family, ministry, or organization—whatever God has called you to.

Nehemiah spent roughly 12 years in Jerusalem overseeing the building project and serving as governor. After the work was completed, he returned to Persia and resumed his role as cupbearer to the king. Then Nehemiah asked permission of the king of Persia to return to Jerusalem so he could see how things were going (verse 6).

We don't know for sure how long Nehemiah had been back in Persia and away from Jerusalem, but most Bible scholars believe it was about ten years. And during those years, the moral and spiritual climate in Jerusalem had greatly deteriorated. Having been granted permission from the king, Nehemiah returned to Jerusalem and was disappointed by what he found—the people were living in mixed marriages. These were not *racially* mixed marriages (the Bible has no problem with interracial marriage), but rather, *spiritually* mixed marriages. The Jewish men had taken pagan wives from the regions around them.

> In those days I also saw Jews who had married women of Ashdod, Ammon, and Moab. And half of their children spoke the language of Ashdod, and could not speak the language of Judah, but spoke according to the language of one or the other people. So I contended with them and cursed them, struck some of them and pulled out their hair, and made them swear by God, saying, "You shall not give your daughters as wives to their sons, nor take their daughters for your sons or yourselves" (verses 23-25).

Nehemiah was so filled with righteous anger that he beat the men and pulled out their beards! He reminded them from their own history that when Solomon had married pagan women, pagan practices were brought into Israel, which led to a terrible spiritual decline and moral collapse.

As leaders we should not beat people, but we are responsible for the moral condition of whoever we are leading.

A LEGACY OF COURAGEOUS LEADERSHIP

The book of Nehemiah ends on the following note, with this final prayer from Nehemiah: "Thus I cleansed them of everything pagan. I also assigned duties to the priests and the Levites, each to his service, and to bringing the wood offering and the firstfruits at appointed times. Remember me, O my God, for good!" (verse 30).

Let that be our closing prayer as well—that God might remember us for being faithful to do *all* that He has called us to do, so that like Nehemiah, we might leave a legacy of courageous leadership.

CHAPTER 4

HUMILITY IN LEADERSHIP

Daniel Fusco

It's been said that confession is good for the soul but is bad for the reputation.

So here goes…

I might be the last person who should write about humility in leadership.

"Why?" you may wonder.

Because I am not known for my humility. And to be honest, when I told people that I was going to write about humility, a bunch of them snickered. Loudly.

Yet I wasn't the least bit offended by this. No one who knows me well says, "Yeah, Fusco is the most humble guy I've ever met."

But don't just skip this chapter! Over the last four or five years, there has been one consistent theme in my walk with Jesus. Over and over again, in every area of my life. Nonstop.

It's all been about *humility*.

The Lord has been working on me. The Refiner's fire was ignited in my life, and I got real mushy.

Have you ever heard how refiners of precious metals work? They use the right amount of heat to make the metal turn to liquid. Once that happens, all the impurities rise to the surface so they can be removed. After the metal is purified, the refiner can then reshape it, then reduce the heat.

So when God is doing a refining work, He makes you a bit mushier than you used to be. He turns up the heat to soften you. The impurities buried deep within your heart, soul, and mind come to the surface. You cannot miss them. They are easily observable. But God does this so that He can purify you. And so that you can be transformed.

This has been a challenging yet necessary journey for me because if I'm honest, I've never been a humble person. Let me share with you about my journey.

I was raised in New Jersey. Sure, there are humble people in the New York metro, but you need a tough exterior to survive. I was raised in a no-nonsense environment that demanded you keep up. Everyone had their own opinions about things, and no one really minded if you didn't agree. Or if it hurt your feelings. So from my youngest years, I learned to defend myself, my opinions, and my ideas in the face of stiff opposition.

As I traveled through my teenage years into my early twenties, my life without Jesus withered into full-on addiction and rebellion. Not only was I arrogant, proud, and boastful; I was also completely and totally lost. Like all the way lost.

Miraculously, at the end of my college experience, I was radically saved by God's grace. Jesus invaded my life in undeniable ways. I was blind, but now I could see, although dimly. I would love to be able to say, "Man, I got saved! I never did drugs again. I never did anything inappropriate with women." But no, that wasn't my story. I was a train wreck in the process of being changed. Over time, Jesus helped me, by His Spirit, to leave the old ways behind. Praise God! When I finally got my walk with Jesus on track, I was almost immediately invited onto staff at a church.

And now I was on the fast track.

After a few years of serving, I was ordained and sent out to plant a church. First, I headed to my home state of New Jersey and planted Calvary New Brunswick. Ironically, the church was in the same town where Rutgers University is located. I was able to plant a church in the same town where I was both saved and graduated from college!

Then a few years later, I went back to the San Francisco Bay area to plant a few more churches, Calvary North Bay and Calvary San Francisco respectively. Then ultimately, I was invited to Vancouver, Washington, to be Pastor Bill Ritchie's successor at Crossroads Community Church, an anchor church with an enormous legacy of impact in the Portland, Oregon, metro area. I like to joke that Pastor Bill Ritchie was like a regal statesman as a pastor. He was buttoned up and flawless. But I am like the regal statesman's funky nephew who you hope doesn't get arrested. I am in jeans and a T-shirt. And flawed. To use a music analogy, if Pastor Bill is a classical composer, I am a weird avant-garde jazz musician.

Immediately upon my arrival at Crossroads, God started moving in incredible ways. Most churches don't do well in their transition from their long-term founding pastor. But at Crossroads, we were growing through the transition. It was extraordinary, and people noticed. Then I began to be invited to speak at conferences and churches of tremendous influence. I was invited to write books and be on television, radio, and all over social media. Ministry went from zero to 100 in no time flat. Things were moving so fast, it was exciting. But it was also treacherous!

During the journey, I started to realize that I knew how to appear humble. I knew the verses to quote, and I believed those verses. But was I truly humble? My reactions, many of them only on the inside, told a different story. I appeared humble, but I wasn't. I was arrogant and proud. I had a healthy varnish of hypocritical humility. I was deeply convicted by the Spirit.

I finally found myself praying, "Lord, will You please humble me?" Those are terrifying words because they line up with God's heart and purposes. God is happy to teach us humility because He loves those who are broken and contrite. But we learn humility through humiliating situations. It was almost as if God had been waiting for my willingness to do a fresh work.

In every area of my life over the last four-and-a-half years, there's been just one lesson: "Daniel, you need to decrease so I can increase." It has been the most horrific and beautiful, the most profound and confusing season of my life, and I'm so grateful for it.

I share my journey with you because all of this is fresh for me. And in what follows, I am not saying that I have gotten it right. I am deeply in process. I have not arrived. We are all always in the process of becoming with Jesus. As somebody who's on the journey, learning the lessons, taking the lumps, I want to exhort you to the urgency of humility in biblical leadership.

I am going to frame this chapter on humility by allowing 1 Peter 5:1-11 to guide us:

> The elders who are among you I exhort, I who am a fellow elder and a witness of the sufferings of Christ, and also a partaker of the glory that will be revealed: Shepherd the flock of God which is among you, serving as overseers, not by compulsion but willingly, not for dishonest gain but eagerly; nor as being lords over those entrusted to you, but being examples to the flock; and when the Chief Shepherd appears, you will receive the crown of glory that does not fade away.

> Likewise you younger people, submit yourselves to your elders. Yes, all of you be submissive to one another, and be clothed with humility, for "God resists the proud, but gives grace to the humble." Therefore humble yourselves under the mighty hand of God, that He may exalt you in due time, casting all your care upon Him, for He cares for you. Be sober, be vigilant; because your adversary the devil walks about like a roaring lion, seeking whom he may devour. Resist him, steadfast in the faith, knowing that the same sufferings are experienced by your brotherhood in the world. But may the God of all grace, who called us to His eternal glory by Christ Jesus, after you have suffered a while, perfect, establish, strengthen, and settle you. To Him be the glory and the dominion forever and ever. Amen.

Isn't this a powerful text?

This text breaks down into three simple parts:

> Verses 1-4: Biblical leaders are shepherds.
>
> Verses 5-7: Humility is the key to biblical leadership.
>
> Verses 8-11: Biblical leaders should expect opposition.

This is exactly how we are going to unpack the urgency of humility in leadership for this chapter. But before we examine these important points, we need to look at the three reasons Peter gives for his authority to exhort the leaders he is writing to. First, in verse 1, he says, "I… am a fellow elder." So he's talking to leaders, saying, "Hey, I'm also a leader." Second, not only that, he was "a witness of the sufferings of Christ." He is saying, "I was there during Jesus' earthly ministry. I saw Him crucified. I saw what happened to Him, so there's credibility to what I'm saying." Third, he also says he is "a partaker of the glory that will be revealed."

So Peter starts by exhorting elders. He is exhorting leaders like us. I love the fact that Peter even says, "Hey, listen, this is *why* I'm going to exhort you." In this chapter, I want to exhort you the way Peter does. I'm also an elder, even though I'm relatively young and dashingly handsome (wink, wink). I know that by the grace of God, I am a partaker in His glory by sheer grace because of the finished work of Jesus. So I hope that you will receive this exhortation from a fellow elder and participant in the work of God's kingdom.

BIBLICAL LEADERS ARE SHEPHERDS

Peter begins with great force. "Shepherd the flock of God which is among you, serving as overseers" (1 Peter 5:2).

Now, the shepherding metaphor was common in their culture, but it's not so common today. The Jewish people were known primarily as shepherds. Remember, toward the end of the book of Genesis, Joseph kept the children of Israel away from the Egyptians because the Egyptians looked down upon shepherds. David, the great warrior king, was a shepherd. He was tending his father's flocks when Samuel arrived to anoint one of Jessie's sons as the next king of Israel. David also told of how he protected sheep from both lions and bears.

I don't know if any of you have sheep. I live in a place where people have sheep and alpacas, and all sorts of other unusual animals. We who live in the Portland metro area pride ourselves on being weird like that. Personally, I do not own any unusual animals, other than our amazing kids. But the job of a shepherd is to protect, to feed, to nurture, and to care for those who are entrusted to them. Really, the best picture of biblical leadership is a servant. To be a servant leader is to be a shepherd.

We must remember that any word picture is bound to have imperfections. A human shepherd with actual sheep is not exactly the same as a pastor or leader who is caring for other humans. Yet, although imperfect, this is still a great picture for us because our job as biblical leaders is to care for people. Whether we run a business or lead a church, our job is not only to be productive, or profitable, or popular. Our job is to nurture people. That is biblical leadership—nurturing people.

So the simple question for us, the litmus test for our leadership, is this: Are people being cared for, nurtured, fed, and matured under our leadership?

Now, don't miss that we are exhorted to "shepherd the flock of God which is among you." This really challenged me, and I hope you hear Peter's challenge. Looking over my years in leadership, I have found myself not always focusing on who was actually in front of me. At times, I was trying to shepherd the flock who used to be there. Or the flock who I wished was among me. Or someone else's flock. I have not always been satisfied or content to focus on the people who are right in front of me. So Peter's exhortation hits home for me.

Are you doing that? We are to shepherd the flock that is among us presently, and we are to do it faithfully.

To be a shepherd, we need to be present with the people right in front of us. This can be a great challenge because leaders are constantly being asked to look ahead and lead. So even as we seek to forecast and evolve with all the challenges and changes of leadership, we must commit to being present with the people entrusted to us.

When I think back over my last 12 years at Crossroads Community Church, I realize that I have pastored five different churches, although they are all Crossroads. First, there was the church that I was invited to lead. As I mentioned earlier, I was asked to be Bill Ritchie's successor in 2012. The first flock I shepherded was the church that I arrived at in 2012.

Almost immediately after I assumed the lead pastor role in the spring of 2013, Crossroads began changing, and quickly! Unfortunately, there were some people who would never let "the dreadlocked guy" be their pastor. I'm not sure that I blame them. I also made some unpopular decisions. And there were *a lot* of new people coming. In addition, there were the inevitable changes in the staff. Pastors were sent out to start churches. If one thing was a constant in that season, it was change.

By the time we hit around 2017, we were at the third version of Crossroads. Things we had been working on for years were bearing tremendous fruit. From 2017 to 2020, Crossroads was growing like gangbusters. Things were exciting and were in harvest mode.

And then...well, you know what happened.

The pandemic.

Even writing that word makes me feel weird.

Life got extra challenging. And very quickly.

The pandemic version of Crossroads was the fourth flock I was asked to shepherd. That was a long and challenging process. Again, there were a ton of transitions. Many people moved away. Others went to churches better aligned with their politics. Some went home to be with Jesus. There was a tremendous shaking and scattering taking place. There were many transitions on the church's staff. Another season of change.

And now, as I write this in 2024, I am pastoring the fifth flock that is among me at Crossroads. We are experiencing a great season again. Crossroads is rocking and blossoming. There is fruit everywhere, and God is moving in our midst. I praise the Lord for that!

But there were times when I caught myself trying to shepherd a flock that used to be among me. Or a flock I hoped would return. Or a flock I hoped we would become. First Peter 5:2 continues to challenge me to be present with the people who are here, now, as they are.

It is also important for us, as shepherds, to remember that we should seek to shepherd our communities as well. We must keep ourselves involved locally, meeting the needs and struggles in our towns and cities. It breaks my heart that many ministry leaders are content to exist apart and separate from their communities.

As Peter continues in the passage, he unpacks for us ways that we shouldn't shepherd. He explains to us the wrong motivations and reasons for leading. It is important that we take heed to his challenges: "Not by compulsion but willingly, not for dishonest gain but eagerly; nor as being lords over those entrusted to you" (1 Peter 5:2-3).

Peter is saying, in effect, "Don't lead because you have to. Instead, lead because you get to."

These challenges speak to our motives. Are we willing and excited to serve God by serving people? Are we eager to serve God by serving people without any sort of compensation, be it status or financial? Are we committed to truly serving God by serving people as a humble servant?

These questions are challenging because they get to the heart of *why* we serve. They focus on potential red flags in our motives. You may have heard it said that God is more concerned with the minister than the ministry. God's desire is that we serve and shepherd with pure and holy motives.

We must remember that money and power can be seductive for humans. Peter reminds us of the wisdom found in Proverbs: "Keep your heart with all diligence, for out of it spring the issues of life" (4:23). We must make sure we are doing God's work in God's way.

Then Peter reminds us, "And when the Chief Shepherd appears, you will receive the crown of glory that does not fade away" (1 Peter 5:4). We are reminded that our leadership is temporary. We do our work in Jesus' place until Jesus' return. We are His hands and feet in our leadership. All our work is done as an extension of who He is. That is why if we are not careful, we can hurt people. But when we faithfully shepherd God's people, there is a glorious reward.

We must never forget that Jesus Himself is the ultimate Shepherd. "I am the good shepherd; and I know My sheep, and am known by My own" (John 10:14). As we follow Jesus, and are shepherded by Him, we will learn the art of shepherding.

As we continue our way through 1 Peter 5, now it is time for us to focus on humility.

HUMILITY IS THE KEY TO BIBLICAL LEADERSHIP

Let's start by defining our terms. Humility is a disposition of the heart that acknowledges that God is God, and we are not. It acknowledges that God is sovereign, and we are not. It acknowledges that God is perfect, and we are not. Humility is a way of living, first before God, that ultimately overflows to people. Humility is what God does, on the inside of us, that gives what we do outwardly a quality that reminds people of Jesus.

I love that Peter wrote this section of 1 Peter 5. If there was one apostle who would not have gotten the trophy for being the most humble, it was Peter. Peter is a textbook "shoot, ready, aim" kind of guy. He's always moving fast. He's impetuous. He's zealous. Almost everything that Peter did before the day of Pentecost, and then also some things after the day of Pentecost, was done recklessly. Remember how Paul called him out in the letter to the Galatians for playing the hypocrite? (Galatians 2:11-12). Peter had liberty to eat with Gentile believers, but when the Judaizers came around, he separated himself from those same family members. Paul had to call him out before the whole church.

And that is just one example of Peter's many documented follies!

But look at how Peter talks about humility. He says this in verse 5: "Likewise you younger people, submit yourselves to your elders. Yes, all of you be submissive to one another and be clothed with humility, for 'God resists the proud, but gives grace to the humble.'" That final sentence is a quotation from Proverbs 3:34.

I love how the Scriptures are always relevant. There is a lot of discussion today, in our culture and in the church, about the exercise of power and authority. And Peter jumps right into the fray with his usual reckless abandon.

"Younger people, submit yourselves to your elders." Every older leader stands up and applauds this statement. But then the next sentence says that *all* of us should be submissive to one another. And every younger person stands up and applauds.

In the Bible, every discussion about submission between people, other than our submission to Christ, is always a picture of mutual submission. Let me say that again: Other than with Jesus, all of our relationships should picture mutual submission.

Our culture loves to rail on Ephesians 5:22. Critics only notice what they believe to be an asymmetrical power imbalance between husbands and wives, men and women. "I could never be a Christian—it says wives submit to your husbands!" That's my favorite entrance into sharing the gospel. I'm like, "That's crazy, isn't it?" They're like, "That is so offensive, patriarchal." I'm like, "Mmhmm. You know what's cool? You know what it says right before it says that? It says, 'Submit yourselves one to another in the fear of God'" (Ephesians 5:21).

First comes mutual submission, which is then applied to relationships.

I'm like, "Oh yeah, so it says first, 'Submit yourselves to one another,' and it says, 'Oh, and wives, to your own husbands.' But then it gets to the guys and it's like, 'Oh yeah, and husbands, love your wife as Christ loved the church and gave Himself for her.'" Did you catch that? Husbands are invited to die for their wives like Jesus died for the church. And now I'm really rolling, "So could we be honest? Which would you rather do? Would you rather submit, or die?" And they're like, "I think I'd like to submit."

Peter, like Paul, is pointing us to mutual submission in the body of Christ. Then Peter says, "'God resists the proud, but gives grace to the humble.' Therefore humble yourselves under the mighty hand of God, that He may exalt you in due time, casting all your care upon Him, for He cares for you" (1 Peter 5:5-7).

So here's the honest truth about humility.

Grace, like water, always flows to the lowest place.

The Spirit of God, like water, fills the lowest places first.

When you fill up a glass of water, it starts filling up in the lowest place.

What the Bible is saying here is that God can do His most substantial work in those who make their lives the lowest place.

If we were to go around our communities and ask people, "Do you believe that Christians are humble?," they will all say, "Not on your life!" Jesus needs better PR than the witness we have. So He is inviting us to be like Himself, to be humble.

Never forget that Jesus Himself is a bright, shining example of humility. He humbled Himself through His incarnation and through His crucifixion. He reminded us that anyone can come to Him and receive rest because He is "gentle and lowly in heart" (Matthew 11:29).

My friend, what would it look like if each one of us made a commitment to pray, "Lord, in my journey as a leader, I want my life to be the lowest place where Your grace can flow. I want my life to be one of those low places that Your Spirit can fill"?

Imagine what Jesus could do!

BIBLICAL LEADERS SHOULD EXPECT OPPOSITION

Now, you might think that when you are a humble shepherd, everything should go pretty smoothly. I wish that were the case, but Peter tells us a different story. Let's look at our final step together.

> Be sober, be vigilant; because your adversary the devil walks about like a roaring lion, seeking whom he may devour. Resist him, steadfast in the faith, knowing that the same sufferings are experienced by your brotherhood

> in the world. But may the God of all grace, who called us to His eternal glory by Christ Jesus, after you have suffered a while, perfect, establish, strengthen, and settle you. To Him be the glory and the dominion forever and ever. Amen (1 Peter 5:8-11).

Peter knew the cost of biblical leadership. He knew that the work is hard and there are many issues to deal with. Peter knew that the opposition leaders face is real. Let's not forget that Peter died a martyr by crucifixion. Peter spent much time in jail and in conflict.

Whether we like it or not, leadership is hard. There will always be opposition. As leaders, we should expect opposition and not be surprised when we experience it.

Notice the exhortations Peter gives:

> Be sober. To be humble leaders, we must be self-controlled and of sound mind.
>
> Be vigilant. To be humble leaders, we must be watchful and on guard.
>
> Be steadfast. To be humble leaders, we must persevere and show tremendous grit.
>
> Be mindful. To be humble leaders, we must remember that others suffer also, just as we do.

All of these encouragements remind us that we are in a battle. Our adversary is the devil. He seeks to devour us. We are told to resist him. We do that by being sober, vigilant, steadfast, and mindful. We do that by remembering that we do not battle against flesh and blood. We do that by remembering that opposition, both to our desire to be humble shepherds and to do the work of God's kingdom, is not an exception. This is to be expected in the work we do.

Here's an unpopular take: Too many leaders today want it easy.

When the going gets hard, they quit. Sometimes they say it is because they are burnt out. Sometimes they say that they are called to something else. Rather than debate the variables, let's simply remember that biblical leaders expect hardship. We expect issues. We expect conflict. We expect that our enemy hates what we do and why we do it.

And the key is to be humble enough to learn through the opposition. It is way too convenient to blame the devil for every problem. When opposition arises, the humble leader asks, "How have I failed?" "What could I have done differently?" "What wrong assumptions did I have?" "How could I have done a better job?" You see, humility leads us to the hard questions.

Knowing that we are imperfect, with the disposition of a heart that is seeking God, we want to reflect on what is happening and why. Like David the psalmist, we want to cry out, "Search me, O God, and know my heart; try me, and know my anxieties; and see if there is any wicked way in me, and lead me in the way everlasting" (Psalm 139:23-24).

Humility reminds the leader that their biggest problem is themselves. Humble leaders see opposition as an opportunity to reflect on where they are at and how they are moving through the world. Only after doing a thorough self-inventory can the leader begin to see how factors outside of them are creating the opposition.

For far too many leaders, there is the implicit assumption that all opposition is happening to them and they are helpless victims. We know that we are not being humble when we are never at fault. But once we have removed the plank from our own eye, we can see clearly enough to notice the specks in others' eyes.

Now, at the same time, it is equally foolish to neglect to locate the opposition we experience in the spiritual realm. It's not either/or. It is both/and. We have an adversary. The devil is real. Often, the devil utilizes people as part of his opposition. Sometimes, we are that person. That's a tough pill to swallow. But it is honest.

Biblical leaders are to expect opposition and keep on going. They don't quit. They persist. And God is glorified. Just as happened with Jesus.

Once again, we see that Jesus Himself leads us on this path as well. The Gospels remind us of all the opposition Jesus faced. Whether it was His own family who didn't understand what He was doing, or the religious leaders who ultimately wanted Him killed, or the occupying Roman powers who carried out His execution, Jesus faced stiff opposition. When you read the book of Revelation, we realize that even at the closing out of humanity, there will still be opposition to Jesus. But does He quit? No! Jesus humbly keeps on going.

So we have covered three important points:

> Biblical leaders are shepherds.
>
> Humility is the key to biblical leadership.
>
> Biblical leaders should expect opposition.

To bring this chapter to a close, I want to draw your attention to the tremendous promises for leaders here in our text.

> When the Chief Shepherd appears, you will receive the crown of glory that does not fade away (1 Peter 5:4).
>
> Humble yourselves under the mighty hand of God, that He may exalt you in due time (verse 6).
>
> May the God of all grace, who called us to His eternal glory by Christ Jesus, after you have suffered a while, perfect, establish, strengthen, and settle you (verse 10).

The Lord is promising each person who seeks to lead as Jesus would, empowered by His Spirit, that even when leading is hard, even when we fail, ultimately, the work is rewarded. Biblical leaders will receive a crown of glory. Biblical leaders will be exalted in due time. Biblical leaders will be perfected, established, strengthened, and settled. How incredible!

So let's keep on seeking the lowest places with Jesus together!

CHAPTER 5

THE SUFFERING LEADER

Ed Taylor

Recently, I was sitting with a pastor friend of more than 20 years as he shared the challenges and pain of his battle with stage 4 cancer. It was a candid conversation—the kind that's raw, emotional, challenging, and hard.

At some point, he must have seen something in my facial expression or noticed the tears welling up in my eyes. He paused. Then he said, "I know it's not like the pain you've experienced with the loss of a son. I didn't lose a son."

I stopped him. "Bro," I said, "the pain we feel is almost the same. The ways we got here might be different. But the pain is so similar."

We all experience pain in life and ministry. I'm talking about the kind of pain that moves you, shakes you, and makes you stumble. It can kick you in the gut and make you question your calling. It can make you ask whether you want to continue doing ministry. And some conclude, *I don't think I want to do this anymore.*

Ministry is filled with pain—things like prodigal kids, slander, gossip, church crises, and financial difficulties. You may have experienced the loss of a loved one, the effects of a divorce, or a serious medical diagnosis. We experience similar pain even though the paths that got us there differ.

As we serve others in their pain, doing ministry can feel a lot like being a first responder. First responders so often deal with people on the worst days of their lives. That's what ministry is—we're first responders in the spiritual realm, serving even those who otherwise would probably never call us or darken the doors of a church.

It's important for us to understand that we're in this together. We're also broken and beat up. When you walk into a hospital room to pray with a family that is hurting, you may be walking in with your own pain as well. Before you go in, you may have to pause and pray for yourself.

I was born to do hospital visits—it's God's calling on my life. After our son passed away, almost 11 years ago at the time of this writing, the Lord called me back to the places that the enemy wanted to take away from me—like the hospital. Not long after my son passed away, I was asked to do a visit in the same hospital where my son had been in the ICU. I was called to go to a room close to where he had been. I felt like the Lord was telling me, "Ed, you need to go in there. You need to take back the hospital because you belong there, and I'll give you the strength that you need."

Listen, we're in this together. We walk into these crises wanting to help others. But we often find ourselves needing help too. We're also hurting. And you know what happens with hurting people, even in the course of ministry? Hurting people have a tendency to hurt people. In leadership and servanthood, we need to receive the healing that God has for us so we don't do that. We need to trust the Lord with our lives.

There's purpose in our pain. In 2 Corinthians, the Bible says,

> All praise to God, the Father of our Lord Jesus Christ. God is our merciful Father and the source of all comfort. He comforts us in all our troubles so that we can comfort others. When they are troubled, we will be able to give them the same comfort God has given us (1:3-4 NLT).

Life hurts. And when you add serving to the pain that you are already experiencing, it can hurt all the more. When God has called you to serve others who are hurting, you may wonder, *How much more can I take?* I've asked that question. And I've heard the still, small voice of the Lord telling me, "Ed, you're going to be able to take everything that I allow in your life because I'm your sufficiency. You're going to be able to make it."

We can think of ourselves as suffering leaders. But really, there's only one true suffering leader. His name is Jesus Christ—the one who's gone before us. As the Bible says,

> He is despised and rejected by men,
> a Man of sorrows and acquainted with grief.
> And we hid, as it were, our faces from Him;
> He was despised, and we did not esteem Him.
>
> Surely He has borne our griefs
> and carried our sorrows;
> yet we esteemed Him stricken,
> smitten by God, and afflicted.
> But He was wounded for our transgressions,
> He was bruised for our iniquities;
> the chastisement for our peace was upon Him,
> and by His stripes we are healed (Isaiah 53:3-5).

Notice how the Bible puts those two together: transgressions and wounded. Pain is associated with ministry—with love and self-sacrifice.

Jesus invites us into this ministry. And suffering is a requirement for anyone in a position of leadership.

Before someone is hired on staff at our church, they have a final interview in my office. In every discussion, I talk to the job candidate about spiritual warfare. I'll say, "Do you want to join the team? If so, you should be ready for unusual spiritual warfare." The response is always, "Yes, no problem," which is great because I think the team members all walk in with the confidence and encouragement that comes from the Lord.

But spiritual warfare can tempt you to cast aside your confidence in the Lord and stop walking by faith. And the result of walking by sight is that you'll walk by feelings—the feelings of what you're going through in the moment. It's important to remember that while feelings are real, they don't always tell you the truth.

Now, pain itself doesn't make us poor leaders. It actually makes us better leaders. It's when we no longer walk by faith with confidence in the Lord that pain can hinder our servanthood.

Serving and suffering should be included in the requirements for any position of spiritual leadership. Suffering and serving go together; they are part of the package. As you serve, pain will come. And with each new year of ministry will come new challenges and suffering that you may have hoped would end—layer upon layer of pain.

Early on, I learned that some trials have a beginning, a short middle, and an end. A trial could be as fast as swerving to avoid an accident on the way to church. You think, *I'm on my way to church, and I almost got into an accident. But I swerved and I'm okay. Praise the Lord!* Though the trial was scary, it went by quickly. I'm not trying to minimize this kind of trial. But after they've gone by, we're relieved. And we move on.

But then there are trials that have long middles. You're wondering when the end will come. Like Paul on the ship that was tossed to and fro (Acts 27:13-38), you're praying, "When is the night going to end, and daylight arrive?"

If that's where you find yourself now, I wish there was something I could do to take away the pain or remove this season from you. But I can't. However, I can pray and trust that God is going to use that pain in your life and make you the better person He desires for you to be.

As the Bible reminds us, "This is my comfort in my affliction, for Your word has given me life" (Psalm 119:50). I love that. One of Satan's favorite tactics is to wear out the saints of the Most High. But Jesus has gone before us, and He is victorious. So I pray you won't quit.

By the way, *quit* is a word we should never use. Just as we should never use the word *divorce* in a marriage, we should never use the word *quit* in ministry. Of course, there are times when seasons end and when it's time to move forward and do something different. Yet we shouldn't quit, or, as the Bible says, we shouldn't throw away our confidence (Hebrews 10:35). Instead, in those times, we need to remember what Paul told us: "I consider that the sufferings of this present time are not worthy to be compared with the glory which shall be revealed in us" (Romans 8:18).

I've been walking with the Lord for nearly 35 years. Before I became a Christian, I walked into a Calvary Chapel and sat in the back. I didn't want anyone to talk to me. I certainly didn't want anyone to hug me. At that church, they hugged a lot. At the time, I didn't even hug my own parents, let alone someone else. But I sat through Bible study after Bible study. Then God broke through my hard heart, and I was born again. And everything changed.

Out of those nearly 35 years, I've been serving the Lord in one way or another, with nearly 30 of those years as a pastor. Looking back, there were years of joy and hardship, happiness and sadness. If I'm not careful, I can think back with a nostalgic view of the past. I'm prone to use the phrase *easier days, simpler days*. And my wife, Marie, reminds me, "No, they weren't as simple and as easy as you think, Ed. They were just different." And I would have to agree. There were different kinds of pain God allowed into my life to make me the man that He wanted me to be. And today, with all the seasons of pain I have gone through, it isn't easy to look back. Sometimes I can end up discouraged. Like the time when my pastor, Jeff Johnson, went home to be with the Lord. After a valiant battle with cancer for five years, an infection took his life. That was hard to deal with—I faced a lot of pain then.

But I do remember this. When I was saved in 1991, I walked the aisle to an altar call. And I came as the man that I was—broken and beaten up, with a life destroyed by alcohol and drugs. My life had been bad, all the way around.

Then when I was born again, I was willing to go anywhere and do anything for Jesus Christ. I put my trust in Pastor Jeff as he taught me the Bible. My mindset was, *Whatever he teaches me, I trust him. If he tells me to do something that's in the Bible, I'm in. I'm willing. And I'm off and running.*

I have what you might call an all-in personality. It's a personality that's very, very bad for sin, but it's very, very good for following the Lord.

That's my commitment: I want to serve the Lord. God has molded that trait in me and used it. I want to continue to be all-in and used by God to the uttermost. That's my desire.

Back when I was still a new believer, if you had given me a list of the things I would suffer and the pain that would be associated with my walk with Jesus Christ and serving Him, I don't think you could have talked me out of going all-in. Back then, I don't think I would have cared about all the pain that was coming. I would have said, "That's okay. You won't believe what God's going to do."

Even if you had told me, "Yeah, but in three-and-a-half years, you're going to have the worst thing you've ever experienced happen to you. And it's all because of this decision," I would have responded, "I'll deal with that when I get there."

However, if you were to give that same list to me today? My reaction could depend on which day you gave it to me. It could depend on how discouraged I am that day, or what circumstance I am dealing with. Ministry is challenging on certain days.

I wonder what Paul felt—in the darkness—while he was blinded after meeting Jesus on the road to Damascus. Certainly, if there are any all-in men in the Bible, Paul would be one of them. And then a visitor came to him with a message. I wonder what he felt when he heard from the messenger:

> Go, for he [Paul] is a chosen vessel of Mine to bear My name before Gentiles, kings, and the children of Israel. For I will show him how many things he must suffer for My name's sake (Acts 9:15).

What would have happened if we had told Paul, in advance, the many painful circumstances and unexpected twists and turns he would face as he served God? I don't think you could have talked him out of it. A few of the experiences he went through are recorded for us. If you are curious, Paul lists them. But first, let's set the context. In 2 Corinthians 11:22, he wrote: "Are they Hebrews? So am I. Are they Israelites? So am I. Are they the seed of Abraham? So am I."

Do you sense an attitude here? Paul is defending the church. He doesn't want the Christians in Corinth to be ripped off by false apostles who boasted about their credentials. But none of them could compete with his credentials, which included suffering:

> Are they ministers of Christ?—I speak as a fool—I am more: in labors more abundant, in stripes above measure, in prisons more frequently, in deaths often. From the Jews five times I received forty stripes minus one. Three times I was beaten with rods; once I was stoned; three times I was shipwrecked; a night and a day I have been in the

> deep; in journeys often, in perils of waters, in perils of robbers, in perils of my own countrymen, in perils of the Gentiles, in perils in the city, in perils in the wilderness, in perils in the sea, in perils among false brethren; in weariness and toil, in sleeplessness often, in hunger and thirst, in fastings often, in cold and nakedness—besides the other things, what comes upon me daily: my deep concern for all the churches (2 Corinthians 11:23-28).

And what we share with Paul—including his sufferings and the fulfillment of Acts 9:15—is what he expressed in that last phrase: "deep concern for all the churches."

If you do ministry right, you're going to have a deep concern for all churches, not just yours. You may think, *I have enough challenges in my own church*. Even so, as one who serves the Lord, you'll have care for all churches.

When you walk into another church, how can you not begin to pray about what's happening there—about what the pastors are going through, what their wives are facing, and what the hurting saints are dealing with? Your heart is knit together with the men and women who serve alongside you. And it's not just a casual concern, but a deep one. Paul went from being a man who wanted to destroy the church to a man who had deep concern for all the churches.

Alan Redpath wrote about Paul's concern for the church. He said,

> I could not possibly convey to you adequately in the English language the force of that statement. I tried to picture it in terms of being smothered under a blanket, or by being attacked and crushed by some great animal, for he could not have used a stronger word when he said, in effect, "That which bears me down, that which is upon me as an intolerable load, that which is a burden, that which is something that

> I can never shake off day or night. It is with me always. I have no vacation [from] it ever. It is upon me daily. The care, the compassion, the concern of all the churches."[1]

Some of the greatest joy and happiness I've experienced has been within the church. God rescued my life and my marriage. He expanded my family and entrusted me with ministry. Some of my most wonderful experiences happened not only in *the* church, but in the church family I serve in Colorado—a family of believers.

But some of the greatest pain I've experienced has been from people within that very same church. People I trusted. People I would have never predicted would hurt me. People I worked with and ministered to. The list can go on and on, just as your list can.

Then when my son, Eddie, passed away in 2013, the revelations of the hearts around us both sustained us and nearly crushed and buried us. I found out who my friends were. I discovered the depth of the friendships of those who were committed to me and my family in our time of crisis. But I also found out who my friends were *not*, and that was hard to bear. Quite frankly, I'd rather not have been crushed by some people. I'd rather have lived in a la-la land of pretend. But that's not real life, and that's not real ministry.

The pain and suffering you're experiencing today are directly related to the strength of your abiding in Christ. If you're serving the Lord in His strength and following in His shadow, you're serving a suffering Servant.

At the time of this writing, 11 years have passed since our son's death. The Lord has been faithful, helping us along the way. But that kind of pain doesn't just go away. It's one of the reasons we're looking forward to the Lord's return. We know that when He comes to rescue His church, there will be no more sorrow, no more tears.

So what can we learn from Paul? What got him through all that he went through? How did he finish well?

I think about my own pastor, Pastor Jeff. He served faithfully—in the same church, in the same community, with the same wife, for 50 years. That's to be rejoiced. He didn't commit adultery, he didn't steal from the church, and he wasn't in the newspaper headlines for the wrong reasons. He finished his race well.

Do you want that? I want that. I know a lot of men and women who are finishing well. And now I have a brother, my pastor, who finished well after serving for 50 years. I saw it with my own eyes. And we should want that to be true of us as well.

How did Paul make it through? How did Pastor Jeff make it through? How will we make it through?

Here's the Word of the Lord to you today. To the suffering leader, to the suffering servant, to the suffering husband or wife, to the suffering elder or child or son or daughter—to the one suffering—the Bible says,

> Do not cast away your confidence, which has great reward. For you have need of endurance, so that after you have done the will of God, you may receive the promise:
>
> "For yet a little while, and He who is coming will come and will not tarry. Now the just shall live by faith; but if anyone draws back, My soul has no pleasure in him."
>
> But we are not of those who draw back to perdition, but of those who believe to the saving of the soul (Hebrews 10:35-39).

You have need of endurance. And here's how you're going to remember that word *endurance*—you're going to remember it as it appears in the original Greek text. You'll never forget it. The Greek word translated "endurance" is *hupomone*.[2]

Not long ago, I did a special service for my pastor. Pastor Jeff had come to our church a couple times, so I took the opportunity to teach our church how to honor our pastors. And the service was great. We saw a wonderful outpouring of God's Holy Spirit.

The following week, a girl came from her Sunday school class to talk to me after the service, along with her mom. She handed me a card with a little cat on it. I told her, "It's so cute. I love your card." And her mom said, "She wanted to give you a little gift."

So I put the card in my Bible and went on my way. Later, when I looked at the card and opened it, there were a few dollars inside along with a little note. At the top, the girl had written in pencil, "Here's some *hupo*-money."

Isn't that great? *Hupo*-money. One day when she hits the worst trial that she's ever experienced, she's going to remember that some pastor told her that God has endurance for her.

You're going to make it through life's painful times because God has endurance for you. God will help you. Sometimes that word is translated as "patience." But I want you to remember the Greek word *hupomone*. Or as the precious little girl put it, *hupo*-money.

The Lord graciously gives us strength for today and hope for tomorrow. God is preparing you for what He has prepared for you. He will give you *hupomone*. Suffering servant, *hupomone* is what you need—bearing up, learning how to wait on God, cleaving to God, enduring, and standing fast. Endurance is at the center of your life. It's how you got through yesterday. And it's how you'll get through today so you can get through tomorrow.

Notice in Hebrews 10:36 the phrase "so that after you have done the will of God." You're going to accomplish the will of God. Although you might delay it, you won't thwart God's plan for your life. I like to say to my church, "You can go the easy way or the hard way." You can try the easy way, but God will sustain you as you go the hard way.

God's kind of endurance means you won't cave in. You won't quit. You won't fall to the schemes of the enemy. You'll keep onward, you won't retreat in fear, and you won't run away. That's the word of God to you right now—*hupomone*.

And if you aren't suffering right now, tuck that little promise into your promise box because you're going to need it. You may not need it today, but one day you will.

Paul said, "None of these things move me; nor do I count my life dear to myself" (Acts 20:24). There are some difficulties that move me, so I'm looking forward to that day when, like Paul, I can say, "None of these things move me." Most things don't move me, but a few do. They challenge me.

Charles Spurgeon dealt a lot with discouragement and depression. He dealt with church issues. He suffered great agony when some people died at one of his meetings because of a false alarm, when someone cried, "Fire!," and a stampede occurred. That incident plagued him for most of his ministry. He was a man who knew pain, just as we do. So when you read Spurgeon's sermons or books, remember that he served—and endured—within a church, even in the middle of great pain.

Spurgeon wrote about how suffering is intertwined with serving. Note what he shared:

> One Sabbath morning I preached from the text, "My God, my God, [why] has Thou forsaken Me?" Though I did not say so, yet I preached my own experience. I heard my own chains clank while I tried to preach to my fellow prisoners in the dark; but I could not tell why I was brought into such an awful horror of darkness, for which I condemned myself.
>
> On the following Monday evening, a man came to see me who bore all the marks of despair upon his countenance. His hair seemed to stand upright, and his eyes were ready to start from their sockets. He said to me, after a little

> parleying, "I never before, in my life, heard any man speak who seemed to know my heart. Mine is a terrible case, but on Sunday morning, you painted me to the life, and preached as if you had been inside my soul."
>
> By God's grace, I saved that man from suicide and led him to Gospel light and liberty; but I know I myself could not have done it if I had not myself been confined in the dungeon in which he lay. I tell you the story, brethren, because you sometimes may not understand your own experience, and the perfect people may condemn you for having it; but what know they of God's servants?
>
> You and I have to suffer much for the sake of the people of our charge...You may be in Egyptian darkness, and you may wonder why such a horror chills your marrow; but you may be altogether in the pursuit of your calling, and be led of the Spirit to a position of sympathy with despondent minds.[3]

Did you catch that? Don't read his words too fast. You and I *must* "suffer much for the sake of the people of our charge."

For those who are willing to experience this, God is ready to move. But we must be willing to obey, count the cost, pay the price, and step into the messes that exist in our communities and our churches so we can be used by God to clean them up. For the pastors and leaders who are willing to surrender, willing to suffer, willing to endure, willing to persevere, great things await. But those who settle on man-made ministry—to please man, to glorify man, to get the accolades of man—you'll never really experience the fullness of what God has for you. Our ministry as a suffering leader is to follow a suffering Savior who died, was buried, and rose again. Our suffering Savior is alive today, empowering each one of us.

One last point: Do you remember when Paul went to God, asking Him to remove the thorn in his flesh? Paul was suffering so much that he begged God for relief:

> Concerning this thing I pleaded with the Lord three times that it might depart from me. And He said to me, "My grace is sufficient for you, for My strength is made perfect in weakness." Therefore most gladly I will rather boast in my infirmities, that the power of Christ may rest upon me. Therefore I take pleasure in infirmities, in reproaches, in needs, in persecutions, in distresses, for Christ's sake. For when I am weak, then I am strong (2 Corinthians 12:8-10).

I love what Pastor Jon Courson wrote about this text. He said,

> The Father says, "You want Me to take away the pain, to solve the problem, to get you out of the situation—but that's not what you need. You need Me. And the very problem you're seeking to get away from, the very situation you desire to get out of is the very one that is causing you to talk to Me, spend time with Me, and depend on Me. You'll be stronger when you're weak because you'll have no other choice than to draw strength from Me. You'll do better when you're weak because you'll have to rely on Me."[4]

Do you know what people value? They value authenticity and honesty. *Authenticity* is a big buzzword today. You know: Be real, true, and authentic. People value confidence, strength, and growth. And that's yours and mine—by faith—through suffering. God is bringing about power, strength, help, hope, and clarity in your life and message because of the suffering He's sustaining you through. God is at work. And nothing is wasted by Him.

CHAPTER 6

LEADING IN CRISES: TWO NECESSARY QUALITIES

David Guzik

The scene was unforgettable: a hospital room with a young couple who took turns cradling their stillborn son.

As a young pastor, I felt that I was in over my head. Of course, I prayed with them and for them, and hoped to speak words of biblical comfort. More than anything, I wanted to simply be there with them, trusting that even my silent presence could help in what was, for them, the worst day of their life.

Thinking back on that day, I hope I did well. The experience helped cement something in my practical experience in ministry. I knew in theory such things happened, but it's always different when a situation becomes reality. Being a Christian leader requires knowing how—or learning how—to help in times of crisis. This kind of crisis is a "normal" part of life in our fallen world.

The year 2020 brought a special kind of crisis for everyone. Our lives were completely upended by a crisis almost no one expected. The global pandemic caused by the COVID-19 virus was bad, but in many ways, the response from governments and institutions was worse. Unfortunately, for many, there is little desire to learn from or reckon with what happened.

Dealing with the pandemic was a special challenge for churches, pastors, ministry leaders, and everyday Christians. Some saw congregants die quickly, often all alone. Others felt the pressure of arbitrary rules that seemed to be more about societal control than sound medical practice. People on every side were riled up, and many pastors and ministry leaders felt that it was impossible to do right by everyone.

Being a leader means making choices that some people won't like; being a people pleaser is never a path to effective leadership. But COVID and the response to it brought a time when many leaders felt there was no decision they could make without angering and alienating many in their congregation. It was like it always is in ministry, only more so.

One pastor in Wisconsin shared how a church member called him "the antichrist" for his views on COVID.[1] This pastor was like many who decided they didn't need the stress inherent in being a lightning rod for such culturally contentious issues. As a result, many pastors left the ministry, or at least strongly considered leaving. The impact was especially deep among younger ministers. During the COVID crisis and response, more than 60 percent of pastors under the age of 35 said they were moderately to severely concerned about their mental health.[2]

As challenging as the COVID years were, it's important to understand that this was, in some sense, an amplification of how ministry and the Christian life always is. Church life and ministry give a high priority to coming alongside people in their crises, helping them with God's truth and God love. In addition to a natural disaster that impacts a community, a war that impacts a nation, or a pandemic that impacts the world, there are the "normal" crises that are just part of life.

Over the years, leaders will face the family with a stillborn child. Another family will experience the sudden revelation of a life-changing scandal. The church community is shaken when a beloved member receives a dreaded medical diagnosis. Sometimes, the crisis is a long-standing problem that refuses to get any better.

For most of us, this is familiar territory. We're not strangers to conflict and crisis; but we don't welcome it. Most certainly, we want to know how to handle it all better. Leadership in crisis is a large topic that has been the subject of many worthy books, so this will be a brief, and hopefully helpful, look at two essential qualities needed in a season of crisis.

These two qualities are drawn from Bible passages that may be less familiar to many believers, starting with Isaiah 50:4-7. These words from the prophet Isaiah remind us that in a time of crisis, we must have a hardened, determined face.

ISAIAH 50:4-7: THE FOCUSED, DETERMINED LEADER

These words come from a broader section in Isaiah (chapters 42 through 53), sometimes known as "The Servant Songs." These beautiful passages speak again and again of God's Perfect Servant, ultimately fulfilled in Jesus Christ.

> The Lord GOD has given Me
> the tongue of the learned,
> that I should know how to speak
> a word in season to him who is weary.
> He awakens Me morning by morning,
> He awakens My ear

> to hear as the learned.
> The Lord GOD has opened My ear;
> and I was not rebellious,
> nor did I turn away.
> I gave My back to those who struck Me,
> and My cheeks to those who plucked out the beard;
> I did not hide My face from shame and spitting.
>
> For the Lord GOD will help Me;
> therefore I will not be disgraced;
> therefore I have set My face like a flint,
> and I know that I will not be ashamed (Isaiah 50:4-7).

As this passage describes God's Perfect Servant, we understand them as messianic prophecies, telling of the nature and deeds of Jesus Christ. When verse 6 says, "I gave My back to those who struck Me," we immediately connect that with the whipping Jesus endured before He was crucified. When we read, "My cheeks to those who plucked out the beard," we understand that this was part of the agony Jesus endured before He was marched to Calvary. In the mention of the plucking of the beard, Isaiah, as God's Spirit-inspired prophet, gave a detail about the suffering of Jesus we didn't know about in the Gospel records. At some time, in some place, there were people plucking out hairs from the beard of Jesus, and as Isaiah wrote, He "did not hide" His "face from shame and spitting." These vivid descriptions of the person and work of the Messiah are part of the reason why some people call Isaiah the Fifth Gospel.

In general, this is a messianic prophecy, and Isaiah 50:7 speaks most directly to the matter of leading through a season of crisis. In our times of great trouble, as we follow Jesus, we must be able to say these words along with Jesus, declaring them to God the Father and to all who will listen.

In Isaiah's messianic prophecy, Jesus said, "The Lord GOD will help Me." Jesus was completely confident in the help that would come from His God and Father. In a time of crisis, as Christ dwells in us, we should be able to believe and say the same. We should be willing to trust God's help, instead of trying to "help" the Lord with our own wisdom and strength.

In Isaiah's messianic prophecy, Jesus said, "I will not be disgraced." Jesus was confident of His ultimate victory and vindication. Though the cross would be filled with suffering and shame, it would not lead to final disgrace. It would lead to the greatest triumph the universe will ever see. As believers, we should have the same confidence in God. We should put away our fears of being disgraced or embarrassed and focus on doing what is right and honoring to God. Even as Jesus did, we should obey God and leave vindication up to Him.

Also in this messianic prophecy, Jesus said, "I have set My face like a flint." As Jesus went to the cross, which was the crisis of all crises, the Savior of the World "hardened" His face. He did not do this in the sense of becoming a hard or angry man, but in the sense of having determination and *focus*, and maintaining that focus through a difficult time.

This idea of Jesus setting His face "like a flint" is of special interest because this prophecy found specific fulfillment in Luke 9:51-56. That part of Luke's Gospel began a new section in Luke's arrangement of the story of Jesus. It began to chronicle the long, final journey of Jesus toward Jerusalem. As Jesus went to Jerusalem, knowing His fate, He did so with utter steadfastness and determination, matching the difficulty of the task ahead.

> Now it came to pass, when the time had come for Him to be received up, that He steadfastly set His face to go to Jerusalem, and sent messengers before His face. And as they went, they entered a village of the Samaritans, to

> prepare for Him. But they did not receive Him, because His face was set for the journey to Jerusalem. And when His disciples James and John saw this, they said, "Lord, do You want us to command fire to come down from heaven and consume them, just as Elijah did?"
>
> But He turned and rebuked them, and said, "You do not know what manner of spirit you are of. For the Son of Man did not come to destroy men's lives but to save them." And they went to another village (Luke 9:51-56).

Note this phrase in verse 51: Jesus "steadfastly set His face to go to Jerusalem." Jesus was focused on His most important work, and nothing would deter Him from that work.

In seasons of crisis and conflict, leaders need to trust Jesus, looking to and relying on Him for the kind of courage and focus that Jesus Himself displayed. It can be said that there are two kinds of courage. There is a courage expressed *in the moment*, which requires no previous thought. This is the kind of instinctive reaction that jumps between a child and danger. This is true courage, but it isn't planned. It is displayed immediately in the necessary moment.

There is also what might be called *planned* courage, which sees the difficulty ahead and steadfastly marches toward it. This describes the great courage that sent Jesus to Jerusalem, then to the upper room, then to Gethsemane, then to His several trials and beatings, and finally to the cross. Jesus knew perfectly well what was in front of Him, and He had told His disciples many times of the cross that was waiting for Him. As Jesus looked out on the horizon, He could see the great suffering and agony He would endure. Nevertheless, Jesus "steadfastly set His face to go to Jerusalem."

When a season of conflict is difficult, you need that kind of courage just to keep showing up. Knowing that some of those who fundamentally doubt you, who inappropriately question you, who spread all kinds of harmful words and thoughts about you, will be at an event takes courage just to be there! They might very well give you the evil eye, a side-eye, and a piece of their mind. Nevertheless, trusting in Jesus, God's leader will stay focused.

When you know that so-and-so will be there, giving you the evil eye and getting in your face, you just want to stay home! But you must stay *focused.*

Luke's description of this in verse 53 shows that the determination and focus of Jesus made some people reject Him: "They did not receive Him, because His face was set for the journey to Jerusalem." When you get your focus, and bring determination to your outlook, some will refuse to receive you. We shouldn't be afraid to follow Jesus down such paths.

Luke also noted that some wanted to distract Jesus with the thought of vengeance ("Lord, do You want us to command fire to come down from heaven and consume them…?"—verse 54). Jesus would not allow His determination and set focus to be turned to vengeance. When a leader has the kind of focus and determined outlook that Jesus had, they may find themselves tempted to strike out at the people who don't support them. This is a trap. Jesus recognized it as a trap, and He rebuked James and John because they did "not know of what manner of spirit" they were of (verse 55). In this different spirit, they were not ministering according to the nature of Jesus. The focus of Jesus was never to "destroy men's lives but to save them" (verse 56).

The spirit James and John showed is often on display in Christian leaders who must lead in a difficult season. They worry about who is for them and who is against them, and what they can do to the people who are against them. That wasn't the focus Jesus had. Jesus was determined to go to Jerusalem and lay down His life as a sacrifice for lost humanity.

With God helping you, don't have the wrong focus during a season of crisis. Your focus shouldn't be damage control, self-defense, political manipulation, or getting even. If any of those things become your focus, and you abandon your determination to obey God and sacrificially love His people and a needy world, then darkness wins the day.

If other people don't share in your focus, they won't understand what you are doing in having a determined face.

You will be tempted to think the battle is with the conflict in front of you: who is going to win, who is going to lose. But the real battle is to see whether a Christian leader can be distracted from doing what is right before God and good for God's people.

If you lose focus, you have lost the battle in your season of crisis. As a principled Christian leader, you should never compromise with error, especially when that error causes harm to the people of God. It's easy to bend to the desires of the powerful and to beg for the favor of the well-known. Yet pleasing other people should never be the focus of a Christian leader, especially in a time of crisis. We should never hope to gain or keep favor with others at the expense of biblical truth, godly character, and simple justice.

It is fair to say that God is focused and determined as He works in the life of a believer. God persistently works toward the goal of conforming His people into the image of Jesus Christ (Romans 8:29). Every believer can be glad that God doesn't lose His focus, and that He is determined to finish what He has started in the believer (Philippians 1:6). As we follow God's pattern, we will serve as leaders who don't lose focus and are determined to complete the work God gives to us.

ECCLESIASTES 7:21-22: THE BLIND EYE AND THE DEAF EAR

The book of Ecclesiastes is often neglected by believers but is filled with nuggets of wisdom for all of us. Here's a great nugget from Ecclesiastes 7:21-22:

> Do not take to heart everything people say,
> lest you hear your servant cursing you.
> For many times, also, your own heart has known
> that even you have cursed others.

I ran across this verse, and this application of it, in a chapter in a book written by the great preacher of Victorian England, Charles Spurgeon. His greatest fame was as a preacher, and not only did thousands come to hear him weekly at the Metropolitan Tabernacle in London, but his sermons were also published through all the English-speaking world and were read by hundreds of thousands of people.

While I appreciate many of Charles Spurgeon's sermons (there are more than 3,500 published sermons by him), I have also benefited from his books. One is titled *Lectures to My Students*,[3] and is a collection of addresses that Spurgeon gave to the students at his pastor's college. In that book, there is a special chapter (at least it is special to me) titled "The Blind Eye and the Deaf Ear."

In that lecture, Spurgeon began by reminding his students that he had often said that he had one blind eye and one deaf ear, and that these were sometimes the *best* eye and *best* ear that he had. He used Ecclesiastes 7:21-22 to explain this, focusing on this line in verse 21: "Do not take to heart everything people say."

The chapter is filled with gems by the quotable Spurgeon, such as this: "You can't always stop people's tongues, and therefore the best thing to do is to stop your own ears and never mind what is spoken. There is a world of idle chit-chat abroad."[4]

Spurgeon described several ways in which a blind eye and a deaf ear can be helpful to the Christian leader. For example, *have a blind eye and a deaf ear when it comes to disputes that aren't your business.* Failure to do this brings a lot of unnecessary trouble. We should remember what Jesus said in Luke 12:14: "Man, who made Me a judge or an arbitrator over you?" If you get involved in disputes that aren't your own, there will never be an end to them. Soon, you will be able to serve and have fellowship with only one group in the church and have to exclude yourself from the others.

This principle has special application in our internet and social media age. We all know there are many things online and in social media that are like quicksand, and will soon consume our time, energy, and defeat our good attitude. Often when others are plainly wrong on social media, it's best to simply turn a blind eye and not feel the need to correct them.

Spurgeon made another application of the principle from Ecclesiastes 7:21-22: *Have a blind eye and a deaf ear when it comes to what gossips are saying.* To paraphrase Spurgeon, the world doesn't have to look far for a source of perpetual motion and renewable energy—we find these in the never-ending work of gossips and busybodies.

It's my belief that gossip is a strange sin in this regard—that apart from a unique work of the Holy Spirit, it is a sin that is impossible to see in oneself. I see it easily in others, but only reluctantly in myself. At the same time, as Spurgeon noted, gossips and busybodies are active. They give a lot of energy to their destructive work and often seem to take pleasure in it.

Yet this is often a place to give a deaf ear and turn a blind eye. We should be like the determined British vice admiral Horatio Nelson. He was literally blind in one eye, and during the Battle of Copenhagen in 1801, he was being signaled by his commanding officer to surrender. Nelson then put his telescope up to his blind eye, looked in the direction of the signal flags, and said, "I really do not see the signal."[5] Nelson carried on, winning the battle.

Spurgeon presented a third application of the "blind eye and deaf ear" principle: *Have a blind eye and a deaf ear when it comes to what others are saying about you.* Many of us are too sensitive to what people say about us. It is a trap for a Christian leader to become like a politician, always casting about to see what others say about us. This has always been a danger, but in a social media world, the danger is much greater. We have a way to quickly see what people "like" or ignore about us and what we think. This obsession with what others think must be fought against. It's not that we don't care what others think of us, but that we have a greater concern for what pleases the Lord.

Too much interest in what others say about us normally results in finding out that they are saying either good things or bad things about us. Each one presents a danger. If you find out they are saying good things, the danger is in believing what they say. Be careful with this. When others compliment you and speak highly of you, it can bear a lot of bad fruit. One danger is that you will begin to believe what they say and start to think too highly of yourself. Another danger is that you may become greatly dependent on these words of praise and come to believe that you have failed when you are not generously complimented. There is wisdom in the old cliché that compliments are like perfume: You should smell them, not drink them. If someone compliments you, especially regarding your Christian service, that's good, and the person who brings the compliment is being kind and considerate. Yet we should hold such praise lightly, and in some sense, present every compliment or "like" in gratitude to God.

The second danger is too much interest in what others say comes when people say bad things about you or respond negatively to what you have done. Sometimes this crushes the servant of God, filling them with a sense of failure, with the thought that their service is of no use to God and others. Also, when people criticize us, it is easy to allow that to change our heart toward the critic. We believe they are out to get us and start considering them as our enemies. This can create much bigger problems. When we treat others like enemies, they will often feel obliged to fulfill the role we have assigned to them. It is both possible and common to take people who are good-hearted critics and push them toward becoming real enemies. Not all your critics are enemies; many of them are friends who can be won over and who really might have your best interest at heart. Treating every critic like an enemy becomes a self-fulfilling prophecy.

Spurgeon told a story of how, when he was a young minister, he received an anonymous letter every week criticizing his Sunday sermon down to the smallest detail. His unknown correspondent picked apart how young Spurgeon pronounced words, when he used an illustration too many times, and other such relatively minor matters. Spurgeon said his only regret regarding those anonymous letters was that he never knew who to thank for the honest feedback. He made it clear that he didn't agree with every criticism the letter-writer offered, but reading those letters and thinking them through made Spurgeon a better preacher. If he had regarded the man as an enemy and ignored everything he wrote, then Spurgeon would have missed a great opportunity to improve his preaching.

It has been said that Christian ministry is a full-contact sport. There are many metaphorical bumps and bruises for those who serve the Lord. In Christian service, we will sometimes be spoken against and lied about. We will sometimes be let down by those who should have supported us. We will endure what seem to be senseless and painful divisions. Those close to us will leave, and sometimes they will leave in unhappy and painful ways.

Because of this, it is possible for the Christian leader to become calloused and defensive. Perhaps the young pastor began very idealistically, but over the years has endured a lot of hurt in the ministry. Maybe some of that hurt was of his own making, and some of it wasn't. Either way, the result can be a hardening of the heart, of the soul toward others. Unconsciously, a dangerous thought dominates: "I'll never let myself be hurt like that again." This self-protective instinct toward others is understandable, but is something of a poison for the servant of God. Spurgeon said it well: "It would be better to be deceived a hundred times than to live a life of suspicion."[6]

The suspicious, self-protective at all costs "I'll never be hurt again" leader is a miserable creature.

Though we hope to never be hurt or betrayed, it will happen. Yet we are called to live, lead, and act toward others as if it never will. The one who can't do this is deprived of the blessings of deep relationships and their isolation from others will contribute to poor leadership. "I'll never trust anyone again" leads to a shallow, sad, and lonely life. When we don't trust others, they can sense it—and they will refuse to trust us. They can sense something is broken inside. Leaders need to remain vulnerable, knowing the risks involved, and be quick to take their hurts to God.

Spurgeon said this to the suspicious servant of God: "Brethren, shun this vice by renouncing the love of self. Judge it to be a small matter what men think or say of you, and care only for their treatment of your Lord. If you are naturally sensitive do not indulge the weakness, nor allow others to play upon it."[7]

A final application of the principle of the blind eye and the deaf ear regards *defending yourself against false accusations*. Leaders put themselves out front, and therefore receive a lot of fire—both from the enemy and "friendly fire." There are times when it is right to defend ourselves against accusations and misunderstandings, but most of us do this far more than is necessary or appropriate. Sometimes we must accept that we will be misunderstood.

One of the first things we know about Jesus is that He was misunderstood. When Joseph and Mary inadvertently left Him behind in Jerusalem, they didn't understand that He had to be about His Father's business (Luke 2:48-50). Jesus was also misunderstood near the end of His earthly life, when those around the cross didn't understand what He meant when He cried out to God the Father using the words of Psalm 22:1 (Mark 15:34-35).

Jesus knew what it was to have His *motives* misunderstood. He healed people, and others said He did it by the devil. He reached out to sinners, and people called Him a drunkard. If you are a Christian leader following in the footsteps of Jesus, expect to sometimes have your motives misunderstood.

Jesus knew what it was to have His *words* misunderstood. He said, "Destroy this temple, and in three days I will raise it up" (John 2:19), no doubt motioning toward His own body as He said the words. Clearly, Jesus *meant* His own body, not the material temple. Still, people insisted that Jesus spoke of the literal temple in Jerusalem (Mark 14:57-58). Another time, Jesus knew Lazarus was dead and He told others that Lazarus was sleeping. They misunderstood Jesus and thought He meant Lazarus was getting much-needed rest (John 11:11-14). If you are a Christian leader following in the footsteps of Jesus, expect to sometimes have your *words* misunderstood.

Jesus knew what it was to have His *silence* misunderstood. When He first appeared before Pilate, Pilate sent Him off to Herod. When Herod questioned Jesus, the Savior didn't say a word (Luke 23:8-9). Herod misunderstood the silence of Jesus and saw it as weakness and powerlessness. Herod was blind to the power and dignity in Jesus' silence. If you are a Christian leader following in the footsteps of Jesus, expect to sometimes have your *silence* misunderstood.

In all the ways we are misunderstood, we have an abiding refuge in God. Prophetically, Psalm 22:24 tells us this was in the heart of Jesus as a prayer to God the Father, even as He suffered: "He has not despised nor abhorred the affliction of the afflicted; nor has He hidden His face from Him; but when He cried to Him, He heard." Most of those standing by Jesus at His crucifixion misunderstood Him; but His God and Father understood the Son perfectly and answered His cry.

For all these reasons, when we are falsely accused or misunderstood, often (not always), the right thing to do is to turn a blind eye and a deaf ear and commit ourselves to God. It's often true that the more we defend ourselves, the more we move away from the nature of Jesus and a simple reliance on the Lord to defend us.

Aren't we happy that Jesus turns a blind eye and a deaf ear to many of our faults and failings? If Jesus were to call us to account for every way we fall short before Him and His holy standard, we would be turned to dust instantly. God knows our every fault and failing, but He patiently works with us and knows in what order things should be addressed in our spiritual growth. There are many things that Jesus sees in us, and He says, "I have other priorities in your life right now; let's deal with it later."

This is principle every Christian leader must live out. There are many times in the leadership God calls us to live out that we will need to have a face like flint, hardened in determination to obey and honor God. There are other times when we must choose to have a blind eye and a deaf ear.

Because these are qualities that are in God Himself, we don't have to work them up in the energy of self-effort. Every Christian can rest in the truth that the best *Christian* to ever walk this earth lives inside them. As Christ dwells in us (Colossians 1:27), as we abide in Him and His word abides in us (John 15:7), He supplies the life-transforming power to do these things. This is a true principle for every believer, but for the Christian leader, it extends further. The best *leader* who ever walked this earth lives inside you. As you abide in Jesus Christ and lead others as He leads His people, you'll be able to effectively lead through every season of crisis.

CHAPTER 7

LEADING AS YOU FOLLOW

Jim Gallagher

When it comes to growing as a biblical leader, there is a very common yet often neglected subject that's important to address: how to lead when we do not know where we are going. Or, to put it another way, *what to do when we don't know what to do.*

One of the realities of life is that we will face situations we have never encountered before. We will come to a place where our past experiences and our current resources do not provide us with the necessary tools to make decisions, solve problems, or chart a course of action. This difficulty is compounded for those in a position of leadership because others who are facing the same situation will look to the leader for direction. The decisions you make will influence the decisions they make. The steps you take will likely become the steps they take. For this reason, it is essential to learn some basic principles that will help you lead when you don't know where you are going.

AN AGE-OLD PROBLEM

Abraham is one of the most important characters not only in the narrative of Scripture, but in the history of the world. He is mentioned by name more than 330 times in the New King James Version of the Bible and is a key figure of the three largest monotheistic religions of the world, making him revered by well more than half of the world's population. He is the patriarch of Judaism, the father of all who believe, and is presented as an example for New Testament believers to pattern themselves after.

Abraham's importance is directly connected to the call God placed upon his life, which gave him a critical role in the plan of redemption. While many of the details are shrouded in mystery, we know that while living in ancient Ur of the Chaldeans, Abraham heard the call of God. He was instructed to leave his home, family, and culture and head to a land that would be given to his descendants. He was promised that these descendants would form a nation and that ultimately, the Savior of humanity would come from this nation. With such a weighty calling, we might expect Abraham to have received step-by-step instructions along the way, but nothing could be further from the truth. In fact, the New Testament author of Hebrews summarized Abraham's journeys this way:

> By faith Abraham obeyed when he was called to go out to the place which he would receive as an inheritance. And he went out, not knowing where he was going (Hebrews 11:8).

The father of the faith, the patriarch of Judaism, the figurehead of monotheism, led his family on a long-distance journey that would take several decades, and for at least a portion of that time, he did not know where he was going.

If you are unclear about how to lead in your current circumstances, you are not alone. We are all confronted with challenges that we are ill-equipped to solve on our own.

A PERSONAL STORY

When the year 2020 began, churches across America published messages or introduced sermon series entitled "2020 Vision" or something similar, in which they cast the church's vision for ministry for the upcoming year. None of these messages anticipated the events that would soon unfold.

The year 2020 broadsided our church just like it did everyone else. The year began strong with record attendance in our services, a calendar filled with ministry events, and a team of three dozen who were about to embark on a two-week trip following in the footsteps of Paul's second missionary journey. One morning I awoke to a series of texts from team members asking if the trip was still on. They informed me that a flu had spread from China and had made its way into Western Europe. In record speed, media sites became flooded with reports about this crisis. With our trip less than a few weeks away, we called a meeting, during which I boldly exclaimed that I would be making the trip with anyone who still felt comfortable going.

But less than 48 hours later, the world shut down. This began a season of constant change as gatherings were restricted, businesses closed, and public places shut down. It seemed as though the only constant was change, and with each change came an onslaught of inquisitive people looking for direction. After a few weeks of trying to navigate through all the unknowns, I found myself in the yard trimming back some overgrown shrubbery and venting. Sweating in the South Florida sun, I found myself complaining about what was going on. I am not sure if you know what it is like to sense the Lord clearly speaking to you, but for me, this was one of those times. If I had to put it in words, the exchange went something like this: I said, "I don't want to lead in this season," to which I sensed God respond, "Lead." At that moment, I knew I would have to learn again how to lead when I didn't know where I was going.

ENOUGH ABOUT THE PROBLEM, LET'S GET TO THE SOLUTION

The Old Testament book of 2 Chronicles records the life and reign of King Jehoshaphat of Judah. Jehoshaphat was like many of us. He was not a perfect leader, but he was a good and godly man who wanted to see revival and reform within his nation. While doing his best to lead, he was suddenly and unexpectedly confronted with a challenge he was not prepared for. His past experience and his present resources did not provide him with the tools necessary to solve the problem.

Three nations that bordered Israel to the east combined their forces, marched into the southern region of Judah, and made their way as far north as the oasis of En Gedi. When Jehoshaphat received the news, he gathered the nation and gave what we might call a State of the Union Address. He explained the conditions the nation was facing and the steps his leadership team would take to resolve these issues. In this case, the king spent less time talking to the people and more time talking to God about the situation. His prayer is summed up this way:

> O our God, will You not judge them? For we have no power against this great multitude that is coming against us; nor do we know what to do, but our eyes are upon You (2 Chronicles 20:12).

In this statement we find the solution to the problem of how to lead when we don't know what to do. Notice there are two parts to the solution. First, there is a realization that we do not know what we are doing, and second, there is a recognition that God does. Most of us realize the first part. We face something we have never faced before, and we recognize we do not know what to do. But instead of looking heavenward, some of us lean into our natural strengths and attempt to engineer a solution, while others simply give up. Typically, there are three types of leaders during confusing seasons:

The Leader Who Lays Down

This is the individual who allows the difficulty they are facing to overwhelm them. Consequently, their tendency is to give up. They are like the person who comes to a steep incline and decides it is better to stop traveling than try to overcome such an obstacle. I have to confess this is my basic nature. There have been many times over the course of my life and leadership when I felt like giving in rather than going on. In the early years of pastoring, I found myself face to face with circumstances I felt ill-prepared to resolve. These difficulties exposed my inabilities, which caused me to question my calling. One Sunday morning, being particularly plagued with my weakness, I pulled my wife aside and declared, "I quit. I am going to tell Anthony [one of our deacons] that he is teaching, and we are leaving." To my surprise, my wife grabbed my shoulders, shook me gently, and declared, "You are in the flesh. That is not what God wants from us. Get in there and teach." Clearly, I needed to learn how to lead when I didn't know what to do.

The Leader Who Leans In

The leader who leans in is the one who looks to their own resources or natural abilities to solve the problems they are facing. They attempt to engineer a solution no matter what. They might echo sentiments like, "God gave us a brain, and we need to use it," or "Any decision is better than no decision." This approach has created unnecessary drama for saints through the ages. Consider Jacob, who, rather than waiting on God to direct him, took matters into his own hands, dressed as if he were Esau, and deceived his father. Rather than solving the problem at hand, Jacob's actions only created drama within his family and forced him to flee for his life. It would take a night of wrestling with God and a lifetime of limping for Jacob to learn not to lean on his own understanding but to learn to look to God.

The Leader Who Listens

This is the leader who understands that while they do not know what to do, God does. This is the person who, when facing challenges, learns to look to the Lord and wait upon Him. In Psalm 32, David provides a very astute insight into leadership:

> I will instruct you and teach you in the way you should go;
> I will guide you with My eye.
> Do not be like the horse or like the mule,
> which have no understanding,
> which must be harnessed with bit and bridle,
> else they will not come near you (Psalm 32:8-9).

Notice the warning not to be like a horse or a mule. I am no expert on the behavior of domesticated animals, but it seems to me the base nature of mules is not to move. You have likely heard the adage, "He is as stubborn as a mule." In this case, we might think of the mule as an illustration of the leader who lies down. Here in Psalm 32, David says, "Don't be a mule." Conversely, the base nature of horses might be to run free. Horses must be corralled. If a gate is left open, horses will take flight. In this case, we might think of the horse as an illustration of the leader who leans in. Left to themselves, they are going to run in their own abilities. David exhorts us not to be a horse.

Instead of lying down or leaning in, David exhorts us to draw near to God and allow Him to lead us with His eye. God knows where He is going and what He is doing. The more in tune we are with Him, the more clarity we will have as we seek to lead others. The leader who listens is the one who recognizes that while we might not know what to do, God does.

Years ago, while sitting in a Bible study, I heard the most remarkable statement. The pastor declared, "The real problem you are facing is that your God is too small." That struck me, and my mind began to be filled with examples of people facing big problems and choosing to reflect upon how God is so much bigger. In his autobiography, the fourth-century church father Augustine wrote:

> For who is Lord but the Lord?
> Who is God except our God?
> The highest.
> The most good.
> The most mighty.
> The most omnipotent.
> The most merciful, yet most just.
> The most hidden, yet most present.
> The most beautiful, yet strongest.
> The stationary, yet incomprehensible constant.
> You cannot change, yet You change everything.
> You are never new, yet never old.
> You make all things new…
> You are ever working, yet ever at rest.
> You are still gathering yet You lack nothing…
> You receive what You found yet had never lost…[1]

I love this prose as it lifts God from the pages of Scripture into the daily life of Augustine and consequently to me. Whatever difficulty he may have been facing, his God was big enough for the challenge.

This is the main ministry principle: *If you don't know what to do, lean into the One who does.*

APPLYING THE SOLUTION TO REAL-TIME LEADERSHIP

If you are anything like me, you know there is a big difference between knowing what a tool is and knowing how to use it effectively. I recently did a small remodeling project that required drywall repair. I know what the proper tools are. I can pick out a trowel, a knife, tape, mud, and even a rasp. But when it comes to doing the job, no matter how slowly and carefully I work, the results still come out looking amateurish.

In the same way, knowing that I should look to God when I don't know what to do and actually putting that into practice are two different things. Perhaps looking at how Paul led a team through a season when he did not know where he was going will prove beneficial to us.

The story of Paul's second missionary journey begins at the close of Acts 15 with his desire to venture out, strengthen the churches, and take the gospel to the unreached. Right away, this venture was plagued by challenges. Paul and Barnabas, longtime friends and co-laborers in the gospel, were unable to agree on whether Mark should accompany them. The result was that two teams developed. Barnabas and Mark set sail to the island of Cyprus, while Paul and Silas headed east toward the region of Galatia.

In Acts 16, upon arriving in Galatia, Paul and Silas spent time strengthening the churches. It is there they came into contact with a young man named Timothy. After inviting Timothy to join the team, they departed from Lystra, desiring to take the gospel to the unreached. This is where more challenges arose.

> Now when they had gone through Phrygia and the region of Galatia, they were forbidden by the Holy Spirit to

> preach the word in Asia. After they had come to Mysia, they tried to go into Bithynia, but the Spirit did not permit them. So passing by Mysia, they came down to Troas (Acts 16:6-8).

While this is a relatively easy passage to read, it would be a very difficult experience to endure. The small team ventured out from Lystra, heading west, with the likely goal of reaching the city of Ephesus. Their plans changed abruptly when Paul sensed the Spirit of God forbidding them. As a result, they headed north toward the region of Bithynia, but once again the Spirit did not permit them. A turn to the east would have taken them home, and if they headed south, they would have ended up in the Mediterranean Sea. Their only course of action was to continue in more of a northwest direction until they ran out of land on the shores of Troas.

Imagine being young Timothy and having just joined the ministry team. You might be wondering whether your leader has any idea what he is doing. One day it is west, the next day it is north, followed by several days with no direction whatsoever. While Paul may have been unclear about where he was going, he was not unclear about what he was doing.

This brings us to our first point of application:

When you don't know what to do, do what you have been called to do.

Today it is common in the business world to talk about mission, vision, charters, and core values. For any business to be successful, the people within must define who they are and stay true to that definition. When a business loses sight of its objectives, it succumbs to "mission drift."

The church has been given a heavenly charter or mission. This is not something we develop on our own; rather, we discover it in the pages of God's Word. That mission is to reach the lost, disciple the saved, and equip the saints for ministry. Everything the church does must be filtered through that charter. It is critical that church leaders do not allow confusing times to distract them from the mission of the church. Political turmoil, social unrest, and environmental calamities may provide opposition or open doors, but we must remain focused on what God has called the church to do.

Paul and his team might have been confused about where to go, but they were not at all confused about what they were called to do. They left Antioch to strengthen the churches, and they left Lystra to reach the lost. The question was not *what* to do but *where* God was calling them to do it. This seems to be a lesson Paul learned early on in his walk with God. On the day he first met Christ, he was instructed to go to the city of Damascus. Not until after arriving in the city would Paul receive directions for the next step in the journey.

What has God called you to do? Are you a student? Be faithful to your studies. Are you a husband? Love your wife. Are you a parent? Seek to raise your kids to follow and serve Christ. If we can determine what God has called us to do, we can fall back on that while we await further directions on where to go.

When our oldest son turned 18, he was struggling to determine the plans God had for his life. He had spent his teenage years as a musician and a competitive surfer and was contemplating whether either of those might be the direction his future would take. On a trip to Southern California, he was attending a local church when he sensed the Spirit of God speaking to him. The message was simple: "Do what is right in front of you, and I will take care of your future." Upon his return, he made himself available to the youth pastor of his church and began helping to lead the services. Less than three months later, the youth pastor moved on, and the next step for our son's journey began. He spent more than a decade faithfully serving as the student ministry pastor.

If you are unclear on what God is calling you to do, remain faithful to what you are currently doing. Jesus taught His disciples that we must be faithful in the little things if we are to be entrusted with greater things. God desires to use your current circumstances to further His kingdom.

> Passing by Mysia, they came down to Troas. And a vision appeared to Paul in the night. A man of Macedonia stood and pleaded with him, saying, "Come over to Macedonia and help us." Now after he had seen the vision, immediately we sought to go to Macedonia, concluding that the Lord had called us to preach the gospel to them (Acts 16:8-10).

Upon arriving in Troas, Paul had a vision. In the biblical storyline, visions are a relatively common way that God speaks to His people. Many of the Old Testament prophets were directed through visions. Joel promised a time when God would pour His Spirit out on all flesh, and dreams and visions would become ways through which God would speak to and direct His church.

With that in mind, let's take a closer look at Paul's vision:

> A vision appeared to Paul in the night (Acts 16:9).

Here, Luke includes the simple little prepositional phrase "in the night." Visions happen when we are awake, and dreams happen when we are asleep. While Paul should have been sleeping, we find him lying awake. Why? Perhaps it is because he was leading a team, and he didn't know where he was going. It is likely that the uncertainty of leading through challenging circumstances put pressure upon Paul that was robbing him of his sleep.

This brings us to our second point of application:

When you don't know what to do, you should seek God more.

Think of it this way: In times of confusion, does it make sense to seek God less? Of course not. The confusing seasons should press us toward the Lord.

I've heard anxiety described as "the soul's cry for God." Just as the body cries for nutrients when it is hungry, so the soul cries out to God when it is frightened, confused, saddened, or weak. In a similar way, confusion in leadership should press us to recognize our need to seek God.

Mark 9 records the story of when several of the apostles faced a demon-possessed child and were unable to deliver him. When Jesus arrived, He cast out the demon. Later, behind closed doors, the disciples asked why they were unable to deliver the child, to which Jesus replied, "This kind can come out by nothing but prayer and fasting" (verse 29).

In other words, when their efforts failed, they should have leaned into the Lord even more. In the same way, when your efforts have proven ineffective, you need to increase your spiritual investments.

Human beings were designed by God to be in a constant state of fellowship with Him, and through the cross of Christ, we can be. Yet there are seasons of life that require us to lean into the Lord more. Fasting is one way that we can do that. But we were not designed to live in a constant state of fasting. We can only fast for about 40 days before we die. It is in one of those seasons that we find Paul and his team. Their response was to seek the Lord more, and as they did so, further direction was given.

Are you in a season of confusion? Do you have a team looking to you for direction, and you don't have answers for them? Perhaps it is time to put some of the timeless principles of Scripture into practice.

> Seek the Lord while He may be found,
> call upon Him while He is near (Isaiah 55:6).
>
> Those who wait on the Lord
> shall renew their strength;
> they shall mount up with wings like eagles,
> they shall run and not be weary,
> they shall walk and not faint (Isaiah 40:31).
>
> Draw near to God and He will draw near to you (James 4:8).

Many years ago, I found myself at a crossroads. The challenges of ministry exposed my weaknesses, which caused me to question the call of God on my life. I sought the counsel of a few close friends and mentors whose advice was very encouraging but did not provide the direction I was looking for. In what was more like an act of desperation than faith, I chose to fast and pray. I set aside several days to simply seek the Lord. To be honest, I did not get the answer I was looking for; instead, God began to reveal things in me that He wanted to transform. Once those matters had been addressed, God began to make the next steps clearer.

This brings us closer to our third and final point of application. Once again, consider what happened in Troas.

> A vision appeared to Paul in the night. A man of Macedonia stood and pleaded with him, saying, "Come over to Macedonia and help us" (Acts 16:9).

As we mentioned earlier, within the biblical narrative, visions are a relatively common way for God to speak to His people. However, this is the first record we have of Paul being directed through a vision. This is significant. Earlier in Acts, we read of Peter receiving a vision, after which he was asked to go the home of Cornelius

(Acts 10:17-23). The events that transpired from that vision opened the doors for the gospel to reach the Gentile world. I can only imagine the expectations that would have arisen in Paul and his team as heaven directed them to Macedonia.

Without providing a wealth of detail, we learn that the vision consisted of a man in Macedonia pleading with Paul to come and "help us" (Acts 16:9). The term "help" implies that a work had begun in the city and that Paul and his team were needed to come alongside and provide assistance. This is not the first time in Acts where a work has started and others are invited to participate. This also happened in Acts 8, when Philip took the gospel to Samaria and revival broke out. It was not long before word got back to Jerusalem and the apostles were sent to help in the work. Later, when Barnabas first arrived in Antioch and saw the impact the gospel was having in the city, he sent word to Tarsus and invited Paul to assist him in the work.

It is highly likely that upon receiving the vision to go to Macedonia, Paul and his team would have expectations of great things happening in Macedonia. Let's see what actually happened:

> Sailing from Troas, we ran a straight course to Samothrace, and the next day came to Neapolis, and from there to Philippi, which is the foremost city of that part of Macedonia, a colony. And we were staying in that city for some days. And on the Sabbath day we went out of the city to the riverside, where prayer was customarily made; and we sat down and spoke to the women who met there. Now a certain woman named Lydia heard us. She was a seller of purple from the city of Thyatira, who worshiped God. The Lord opened her heart to heed the things spoken by Paul. And when she and her household were baptized, she begged us, saying, "If you have judged

> me to be faithful to the Lord, come to my house and stay."
> So, she persuaded us (Acts 16:11-15).

Paul and his team stepped off the boat in Neapolis, and there was no one there to meet them. Concluding this was not where God was leading them, they made the eight-mile journey to the city of Philippi. Once again, there was no one there to meet them. After several days without any evidence of any man engaged in kingdom work, Paul and the team headed out to the riverside, where they encountered a small gathering of women who met to pray. The next scene takes us back into the city of Philippi, where they encountered a young girl who was possessed, and Paul cast the demon out of her. While I would never want to diminish the importance of one person encountering the Lord, this is certainly not what Paul's team expected. Whatever expectations they might have had were met with the reality that no real work was happening in the city.

This brings us to our third and final point of application:

When you don't know what to do, look for open doors to further the kingdom.

When Paul and his team found no man working, they went on the lookout for what else God might want them to do. They went to the riverside, they walked about the marketplace, they even found an open door in the county jail. This has always been the way of the church.

In physics, we learn about things that are static and things that are dynamic. Static refers to something that remains fixed or unchanged; dynamic indicates constant movement, adaptation, or evolution. In leadership, it is important to keep in mind what things about the church are to remain static or unchanging, and what things are to be dynamic. If the church fails to preach the gospel, teach the Word, and equip the saints, it ceases to be the church. But from its inception, the church has had to learn to be dynamic in the expression of its unchanging principles.

The church started in revival, creating instant problems regarding where to meet. Church leaders had to be dynamic in their approach about providing fellowship, communion, and teaching. At the same time, the church was also birthed into persecution, and church leaders had to wrestle with outside pressures that were attempting to stop their gatherings and oppose their evangelistic efforts. It is important that we learn to do the same.

Disappointment can be crippling. It is quite common for life to rattle our expectations. This happens in marriage and family relationships, the workplace, and especially in ministry. We think our efforts will yield a certain result only to discover things tend to go very differently than we had hoped or expected. Instead of allowing things outside our control to discourage us, we should see these things as course correctors. Paul and his team thought ministry in Philippi would look a certain way; however, as events unfolded, they soon learned God had a different approach for reaching the city.

In the early years of my ministry journey, my path crossed with that of another young man who was attempting to determine the plans God had for his life. He had been impacted by the stories of missionaries and sensed God was calling him to the mission field. After a handful of years without an open door, he began to alter his approach and even considered taking a position teaching English as a second language to pursue his dream. While taking steps in that direction, he clearly sensed those doors being closed. Not long after this, he stepped into a full-time position as a youth pastor. In less than a year, he became the lead pastor of a local church. It looked as though his missionary desires might not be fulfilled. However, as the calendar pages turned, he discovered multiple ways for his church to engage on the mission field. Now, decades later, their efforts have resulted in missionary endeavors in multiple countries around the world.

Allow me to close with an application from one of the most well-known of all Bible stories: the fall of Jericho. After the people of Israel entered the land of Canaan, their first campaign was to overtake Jericho. The problem was that the city was surrounded by enormous walls and the people within were on high alert. The text explains that the walls were securely shut and no one went in or out of the city. With that scene in your mind, read what the Lord told Joshua:

> See! I have given Jericho into your hand, its king, and the mighty men of valor (Joshua 6:2).

I'm sorry, but if I were Joshua, my response would have been, "That is exactly the opposite of what I see. I do not see a city given over to us, but a city that we are unable to conquer." The story of Joshua is the story of how to walk through a closed door. Joshua, like Abraham, like Paul, and like you and me, had to learn how to lead when he did not know what to do. As Joshua sought the Lord, he was given instructions that might seem ludicrous but resulted in the purposes of God being completed in and through his life.

If you are facing a season of uncertainty, you do not know how to lead because you do not know what to do. But remember that you are not alone. The heroes of the faith went through similar seasons. In your uncertainty, be sure to do what God has called you to do, set aside ample time to seek Him, and look for new and dynamic ways to participate in the furtherance of His kingdom.

CHAPTER 8

LEADING BY BUILDING RELATIONAL BRIDGES

Sean McDowell

Don't practice what you preach. Instead, preach what you practice.

You might think that's counterintuitive. Aren't we supposed to live out that which we preach? About 25 years ago, when I was starting in ministry, my father said to me, "Son, don't be like everybody else and practice what you preach. Rather, preach what you practice." His exhortation has shaped the way I've tried to live out my ministry.

When I started out as an apologist years ago, I noticed there were some people who taught apologetics, some who wrote books on apologetic evangelism, and some who gave talks on apologetic evangelism, but then none of these people were doing what they teach or preach. Then there were others who were engaged in evangelism. They were having spiritual and gospel-centered conversations with others, and their apologetics emerged from what they were *doing*.

That's when I realized I wanted to be an apologist who preached what he practiced. In other words, I wanted to teach others out of what I was doing (or at least *trying* to do).

So let me ask you this question: What kind of leader are you? Maybe you teach or preach, or maybe you don't. But no matter what your role as a leader, are you leading others from your own experience and practice?

I had breakfast with a pastor in Southern California who said to me, "I'm noticing a trend in my church. Most of the people don't view themselves as ambassadors for Christ. They think that's the job of the pastor and other ministry leaders. Their job is to show up, give their offering, and maybe study the Bible when they can. How can I change that? How can I get the people to see themselves as ambassadors and seek to engage their family, coworkers, and neighbors in gospel-centered conversations and minister to them?"

JESUS, THE ULTIMATE LEADER

Before I share my response to the pastor, I want to set the stage with this important question: What makes a leader effective? I believe the key is to identify a problem, discover a workable solution, and motivate people to execute work toward solving it.

That's what a good leader does, and Jesus was the ultimate leader. He recognized the problem of sin, which broke our relationship with God. He came up with a workable solution, which was to offer His own life as a sacrifice. Then through the power of the Holy Spirit and discipleship, He executed a plan that has since influenced more people than any other leader in the history of the world.

That's what made—and still makes—Jesus the ultimate leader. So I told the pastor, "Step one is to identify the problem. Many in your church don't view themselves as ambassadors. If you want your church to do this, you need to do it yourself first. You've got to lead by example. Don't practice what you preach. Preach what you practice.

Lead by example and share your successes and failures. Step two is to train your congregation how to do this. Give them the actual tools. And three, create a climate within your church where people are motivated to be ambassadors and to engage those around them."

WATCH FOR THE OPPORTUNITIES

At Biola University, I teach an undergrad class called "Gospel Kingdom Culture." I talk about evangelism, apologetics, and the thorniest cultural social issues you can imagine. The students learn how to find common ground with people and engage them in spiritual conversations.

I start every class by asking, "Did anyone have a spiritual conversation this past week you can share about?" I do that to create a bit of healthy peer pressure and to foster an expectation that they're doing this.

One time, a student shared about a conversation he had with a woman on an airplane. As they talked, their dialogue shifted to spiritual matters. The woman had grown up in the church but experienced serious abuse, which affected how she viewed God. The student talked with her and ministered to her. Then the student told the rest of the class, "I've never had that kind of door open for me before."

I mentioned to the pastor that nothing had changed for the student. The opportunities for such conversations are always around us. But we need to watch for them and expect them. I suggested that the pastor create a sense of expectation among his church members so that they would be trained to notice opportunities when they arise.

I also suggested that every so often, the pastor should have someone in the church share, with the congregation, their experience of engaging with others. He could then use this as a launching pad to motivate the people in his congregation to be ambassadors for Christ.

Many Christians don't realize that most people are open to spiritual conversations. Why? Partly because they are made in the image of God and eternity is on their hearts. And partly because we live in a culture in which people are hungrier than ever for meaning and truth. The key to reaching out to others is to have conversations in the right *way* at the right *time* in the right *place*. And when we're willing to lean into the opportunities around us, we'll discover the vast majority of people are open to spiritual talk.

REASONS TO BUILD BRIDGES

Now, why should we think of ourselves as ambassadors for Christ? Here are three reasons that come to mind based on conversations I've had with people.

First, I learn a lot when I talk to people who hold to different worldviews. Sometimes doing this helps you to see your blind spots. I once called an imam at a mosque near where I live, and asked, "Can I bring my eleven-year-old son for a tour of the mosque, and can we ask you some questions?"

The imam agreed, and as a result, we started an ongoing conversation and a relationship. Very few Christians have made an effort to reach out and build bridges with him.

Second, one of the best ways to love someone is to listen to them. We live in a culture where people are hurting and want to be heard. In our distracted age, paying attention to someone wholeheartedly is a powerful act of love. Healing takes place when you look someone in the eyes and ask, "How are you doing?," and then you simply listen without having an agenda.

As Christians, sometimes this is hard for us to do, isn't it? This doesn't come naturally to me. I'm a professor, so my job is to have answers. And it's easy for us to get anxious about offering answers without really listening to people.

How wonderful it would be if people, when they were hurting or broken, would think, *I need to talk to a Christian because a Christian will listen to me*. When we listen, we show love and care.

Third, when we get outside of our comfort zone and spend time with people who see the world differently, we will find ourselves changed. Our tendency is to look at non-Christians through the lens of us versus them—whether it's us versus another religion, or political party, or sexual identity, or something else.

Yes, we should stand for truth and proclaim it—absolutely. But when we build bridges with people who hold to different views, we learn how we can be more sensitive to their needs. And that enables us to do better at showing the love of Christ.

I met a youth pastor who was asked, by a public school, to be an advisor of sorts for an LGBTQ club. Most of us would say no immediately. But he realized this would give him the opportunity to interact with and positively influence these unique kids. He said these kids saw themselves as hated, marginalized victims, and asked him, "Why don't you hate us?"

They were surprised by the way he treated them. Rather than quoting Bible passages of condemnation, he started with passages about the person of Jesus. He said, "I first wanted them to be captivated by who Jesus was. Then we could talk about the other issues downstream." He said a few of the young people went on to visit his church, and eventually, a couple of them trusted Christ as their Savior.

I asked the youth pastor, "How did this change you?" He said at first, he didn't recognize his anger toward this community. But as he spent time with them and heard their stories, God broke his heart for them.

When we step outside of our comfort zone and lead by example, it's going to change us as well as others.

FEARS AND MISTAKES

One reason many Christians are hesitant to build bridges is they're afraid they'll be asked questions they can't answer. That's okay—I have two master's degrees and a PhD, and I still face that fear too.

But I discovered three words are empowering and good to say to others when you don't have an answer: "I don't know."

To say that is to be honest. You don't want to give a wrong response that will cause you to lose all credibility in another person's eyes.

What's great about saying, "I don't know" is it gives you the opportunity to connect again later. You can say, "That's a good question. Let me research that and get back to you." This response tells the other person that you're honest and caring, and that you want to continue the conversation.

There's another fear some Christians struggle with: They think that listening to someone who holds to an unbiblical worldview equals an affirmation of that worldview. The assumption is that we should immediately point out another person's mistakes.

But listening to and understanding someone who holds to a different worldview doesn't mean you are affirming them. Don't feel you need to be quick about pointing out your disagreement. Focus on engagement so the door is open for further spiritual conversations.

First Peter 3:15 talks about "sanctify[ing] the Lord God in your hearts, and always be[ing] ready to give a defense to everyone who asks you a reason for the hope that is in you." This brings to mind the rule of reciprocity. If I listen to someone and try to understand their view, they're going to be more motivated to listen to and try to understand my view. In fact, sometimes people feel obligated to do so.

The third reason we don't have spiritual conversations with others is that we don't know how. But after you read this chapter, you'll no longer have that excuse. We're going to talk about this now. But first, I want to share this important principle: If you mess up, the relational content rarely matters.

What do I mean by that? When it comes to communication, you have the *medium* and the *message*. The medium is the means you use to communicate, and the message is the content. The medium could be to write something in sand, or to send a text, or to speak through a bullhorn. You could make a YouTube video or use the written word.

The message is the content—or in our case, the truth.

With that in mind, consider this question: What mediums does God use to communicate His message that the truth sets us free? Psalm 19:1 and Romans 1:20 tell us God uses the medium of creation. He also uses the medium of our conscience (Romans 2:15). Elsewhere in Scripture, God uses angels, prophets, visions, dreams, and more. But God's ultimate revelation—and this is unique to Christianity—was when Christ stepped into our world through the incarnation, or He came to earth in human flesh (Hebrews 1:1-2).

There are two mistakes that Christians frequently make. The first is they'll say, "I'm speaking God's truth. If that offends you, that's your problem." This person has truth but lacks grace and love. The other mistake is to say, "We need to love others and be kind to them and not offend them with the truth." Such sentimentality may be motivated by love, but it lacks the truth that can set people free.

Effective communicators will not compromise truth but will speak it in love (see Ephesians 4:15). And sadly, there are few Christians who do this well.

I know this because of an experiment I do often at churches and conferences—an experiment I call my atheist encounter. I put on a pair of glasses, role-play an atheist, take questions from the audience, and respond as an atheist might.

Usually after 20 or 30 minutes, most people get testy and angry with me. I've had people call me names. I've had them storm out; I've had them cut me off—even though they know I'm role-playing!

Then I take off my glasses and say, "Before we talk about how to defend the faith, how did you treat your atheist guest?"

Yes, I'll push people's buttons when I act out an atheist. And some in the audience will realize they didn't respond so well. They were defensive, aggressive, hostile. One young woman said, "We felt like you weren't a human being. And we were just trying to win an argument and prove you wrong."

I've done this many times all over the world, and it's rare to find a Christian who can ask thoughtful questions with the right spirit. That's what we're called to do—to love people with the right spirit. We're to be thoughtful, asking good questions and engaging with people graciously.

Jesus modeled communicating with others in two primary ways: He told stories, and He asked questions. In the Gospels, Jesus asked 340 questions.[1] He was asked 183 questions[2] and He directly answered only eight. This tells us Jesus saw questions as an effective way of opening communication opportunities with others. With that in mind, I'll soon share four questions you can ask to get spiritual conversations going with others. But first, I want to show how asking questions can be effective for keeping a conversation going.

TAKE THE INITIATIVE

Some years ago, I participated in a debate in the town where I live. The topic was God and morality. Afterward, a professor who taught at the junior college that hosted the debate came up to me. He said, "You're saying that God is the best explanation for moral values. But how do you explain what the Bible says about slavery? It says you can beat a slave."

At this point, I was exhausted from debating for three hours. But I wanted to address his questions. I asked him where he was from, and he said he lived in town. I asked if we could meet over coffee, and he agreed.

One reason I did this is because we were surrounded by others, and I didn't want to end up in a situation where things could get potentially awkward. That's the advice I often give to students. If you have a professor or teacher who is aggressive against Christianity, be the best student in the classroom setting, and be gracious and thoughtful when you ask questions. But if you want to engage in spiritual conversation, do a one-on-one visit with the professor during office hours, and oftentimes you'll see a different person.

When the junior college professor and I got to the coffee place, we sat down. I said, "I'm happy to talk about the Bible and slavery, but I'd like to begin by asking two questions. One, if there is no God, how is it possible for there to be objective right and wrong? And two, how is it that humans have value? If you could answer those for me, then I'll know where you're coming from, and that will help us as we go over Exodus 21 and talk about slavery."

As it turned out, we never got to Exodus 21. But we started a conversation, which opened the door for more opportunities later on. He invited me to a junior college class he was teaching. I was able to speak to his non-Christian students about why a spiritual quest should begin with Jesus, and then answer questions from them.

All that happened because we took the time to have a conversation. There are always opportunities around us if we look for them. We can use these to lead other believers by example, and help them to do the same.

A while later, I reached out to a group of skeptics who meet together, give messages, and do events. I introduced myself to one of them. The guy said, "Hey, I know who you are. I was at that debate here in town."

I told him, "I've written a book that responds to atheism, and I'd love to know what you and your friends think. What if I were to come visit one evening, sit on the hot seat, and let you and your group ask anything you'd like to ask a Christian?"

He said, "You're the first Christian who has approached us." I was surprised. I thought, *Why am I the first Christian willing to meet and talk with them?* What does this say about Christians?

Sadly, he didn't know any Christians. Nor was he interacting with any. This means he didn't have the opportunity to meet with anyone who could counter all the stereotypes he had heard about Christians.

Afterward, I received an email from a student who had been there during my visit. We ended up agreeing to meet and talk. From there, I was able to invite him to church a couple times. I also invited him over for dinner to meet my family. Our dialogue continued, and it all started because of a willingness to sit down and have a conversation. Opportunities are all around us if we would just open our eyes to see them, and then respond.

On another occasion, I reached out to a lesbian YouTube content creator. I thought it would be interesting to have a conversation with a non-Christian who probably thinks a lot of my YouTube content is offensive. I reached out and gave her full disclosure: I told her I am a Christian professor and apologist. I asked if she would be willing to come on my YouTube channel and talk about her journey, and she said yes.

During our conversation, we talked about spirituality. She said she was "into spirituality, and spirituality, for me…it's a lot of different [things]." She then said, "I look at other religions…I think that's the way to do it, like, you take a little from each thing, because they're all very similar, right?"

I said they may be "similar on the edges, but at the core, very, very different." I pointed out that they differ greatly on whether there is a personal God, on what is wrong with the world, and on where we go in the afterlife.

We continued talking. At the end of our dialogue, I asked, "Do you have any final questions [you would want to ask a] Christian professor?" I had no clue what she might bring up. She said she thought her audience would want to know how I would respond if one of my kids were to announce he or she was gay.

I said, "I would look at my son or daughter in the eyes, and I would say, 'Thank you so much for sharing [that] with me. I can only imagine how much time and effort and probably fear it took to tell [this to] your dad…Thank you for trusting me with this. Know that I love you no matter what…and we are going to work through this together.'"

She liked my response, and as it turned out, afterward, there were many in the LGBTQ community who started watching my videos in which I defend the Bible and make the case for the resurrection and deity of Jesus. They were willing to listen because I had expressed an interest in listening first, and had shown kindness and grace.

Again, there are more opportunities than we sometimes realize. We need to watch for them and take the initiative.

FOUR HELPFUL QUESTIONS

Now we're ready to look at the four questions that are helpful for getting spiritual conversations going. These questions come from my friend Tim Muehlhoff, a professor at Biola. They appear in a book on which I was the general editor, titled *A New Kind of Apologist*.[3] Here, I'm going to expand and tweak them a bit. The first one is a great starting point:

1. What do you believe?

From experience, I've learned that it's possible for us to spend too much time answering questions that people aren't asking because we have made assumptions about what they believe. For us to have an effective spiritual conversation with someone, we need to clearly understand what they believe.

That's why it's essential to ask, "What do you believe?" And we can then build on this to continue the conversation: What do you believe about Jesus? About the afterlife? About racism? About this? About that? Asking these questions will help you to understand where another person is coming from.

Proverbs 18:13 says that if someone gives an answer before he hears, it is his folly and shame. It's okay to tell someone you're asking this question—and its variations—because you want to better understand what they believe.

Here's the second question:

2. Why do you believe this?

The more I talk with people, the more I've become convinced that deep down, most of them don't truly understand why they believe what they do. This is often true for Christians *and* non-Christians. They might give what sounds like an intelligent response, but frequently, there is so much more at play.

For example, some time ago, I spoke with a young man who said he had left his parents' faith and was an atheist. As he asked me questions, I was thinking, *I'm having a hard time believing these issues are what motivated an 18-year-old to leave the faith of his parents.*

So I said to him, "I could be wrong, and I apologize in advance if I am. But it doesn't seem like the questions you're asking explain the reason you've left the church."

He said, "You're right. I've graduated from high school, and in the fall, I'm going to a public university. I'm joining a fraternity, and I want to have some fun in my life."

I responded, "So you think Christianity restricts your freedom, and you can't do anything that's fun." Evidently that was the motivating reason behind his rejection of the faith.

Proverbs 20:5 says, "The purpose in a man's heart is like deep water, but a man of understanding will draw it out." When I talk with others, I'm always asking myself, *How do I draw out the real reason for the way a person believes?*

A 19-year-old man once told me the idea behind the Trinity is incoherent. I said, "Theologians in the church have been wrestling with this for a thousand years. Have you read what has been written on the issue?" I then named some books. He said he hadn't read them. I graciously but firmly said, "If you continue to decide the doctrine of the Trinity is incoherent, that's up to you. But if you haven't studied on this, then the real issue here seems to be pride. You say you've got this all figured out at age 19 but you haven't done the research."

When you converse with non-Christians, listen carefully. You may discover that the reason for their objections isn't based on a careful study of the facts. Sometimes the real issue is something else—something relational or emotional or intellectual. They may have been mistreated by a Christian or met Christians who weren't loving. Their experiences or the way they think may affect how they are processing the message.

This is why it's so vital to ask people why they believe the way they do. When you talk to someone, pray for the wisdom to figure out what's at the root of their objections. Ask, "What people most influenced you?" You can't understand a person apart from those who influenced them—perhaps their father, or a schoolteacher, or a coach, or a close friend.

You can also ask, "What life experiences most shaped you?" This can include their experiences with Christians or with the church. This is especially important when you're talking with someone who says they have de-converted from the faith.

Still another helpful question is, "What are your past hurts?" You want to be careful about asking this. But if it's appropriate to do so, it may help your conversation on the relational front. It will show that you care, and that can help to build bridges. And if we want people to share their hurts, it often starts by sharing ours first.

At the same time that you ask, "Why do you believe this?," you can also ask, "What do you think Christians actually believe?" Again, the goal is clarity. Not only do you want to understand where another person is coming from, but you also want to know how they perceive Christians. Do they have wrong perceptions that are affecting how they believe? Taking this path can open the door for you to share what Christians really believe, or what Scripture really teaches.

The third question to ask is...

3. Where do we agree?

During conversations, it's vital for us to find common ground with people. Have you ever noticed how excited two strangers get when they find out they're from the same town or state, or they've traveled to the same places, or they like the same music, sports teams, or hobbies? Common ground helps to bind people together. It builds bridges.

Many Christians are quick to focus on differences when they engage with unbelievers. When the apostle Paul spoke to non-Christians on Mars Hill, notice how he first attempted to build a bridge. He said, "I see you are very religious people." What was he saying? "I see that you're religious, and I am too." To find a point of common ground helps to humanize the conversation. He also quoted their poets *positively* (Acts 17:28).

When you search for common ground, however, you want to be careful you don't compromise on the truth. You also want to recognize that people of other religious often assign different meanings to words that we use. Mormons and progressive Christians use the same vocabulary we do, but often with entirely different meanings behind the words. So you want to be cautious when you search for common ground on spiritual, moral, or ethical issues.

The fourth question is...

4. Where do we differ?

During spiritual conversations, I am always watching for opportunities to share the gospel, provided the person appears to be open or ready. Yet, I don't try to make that happen in every dialogue. I'll try to lead the conversation in that direction, but if the timing doesn't seem right, I'll wait. As Greg Koukl has said, "*All I want to do is put a stone in someone's shoe*. I want to give that person something worth thinking about, something he can't ignore because it continues to poke at him in a good way."[4]

Knowing where you differ with someone will help you to know whether further conversation is possible. For example, I've talked with a number of skeptics about the cosmological argument for the existence of God. The first premise of the argument is that whatever begins to exist has a cause. The second premise is that the universe began to exist. The conclusion is that the universe therefore had a cause. The point of the cosmological argument is simple and powerful: For the universe to exist, it must have a cause outside of it that brought it into existence.

If you trace that argument back far enough, eventually an atheist only has so many options for why there is something rather than nothing. One option is to take an agnostic position. Or they can say the universe has always been here—a view that runs into many problems philosophically and scientifically. Or the universe literally came into existence uncaused.

I remember speaking to one skeptic in particular who believed that the universe began to exist: "In my worldview, I have a cause outside of space and outside of time that can bring the universe into existence. In your worldview, you have to believe that it's possible for something to come into existence out of nothing. Do you think something from nothing is more reasonable?" He looked me in the eyes and said, "Something from nothing is more reasonable." At that point, we had clearly articulated our differences. He believed the universe can be uncaused, and I believe it needs a cause. We got to the core differences in our beliefs about the origin of the universe and stated them clearly.

Clarifying differences can be powerful. In one case, a skeptic became a believer about a decade after we discussed the cosmological argument. He admitted to me that he had a slight doubt that the universe could appear uncaused. But it took time and a long season of relationship for him to reach that point. I've seen many former Muslims and atheists take years to come to Christ.

Do we lean in and build relationships? Do we ask good questions? Do we look for common ground? That's what good leaders need to do. They need to lead by example, then preach what they practice.

WHEN DISAGREEMENTS ARISE

When we talk with unbelievers, we are sure to have times when we're uncertain about how to navigate a spiritual or moral point of disagreement. Some issues are more complex than others, and we are unsure of where to draw the lines when it comes to our convictions.

When that happens, here are two principles I hope are helpful.

One, it's important to separate secondary issues from primary issues. By primary or essential issues, I mean those that are salvific, or that relate to a person's salvation. These are the issues we need to stand firm on. Spiritually, the Bible is clear about the resurrection of Jesus and salvation by grace alone. Morally, the Bible is firm on God's design for marriage. These are among the essential issues we cannot compromise on.

And two, we need to show a biblical love for people. This kind of love speaks the truth. But what do you do when it comes to the gray areas that the Bible doesn't address directly? You might have strong feelings about certain gray areas, but we have to recognize some issues aren't directly addressed in the Bible.

For example, the Bible doesn't talk about gun control. But it does talk about the value of life and loving our neighbor. Scripture also says that love protects others. We can apply these principles to guide us in discussions about gun use or self-defense.

When we take a firm stand on an issue, we have to ask ourselves if we are dying on the right hill, so to speak. We need to pay careful attention to how we treat others and to be gracious and charitable when we state our convictions without compromising them.

Those two principles—primary versus secondary issues and showing biblical love—can help guide us as we navigate areas of disagreement. We see a great example of this played out in Scripture. When Daniel and his friends were taken captive in Babylon, they were told to eat the food provided by King Nebuchadnezzar. Daniel was wise. He didn't immediately rebel when he and his friends were ordered to eat the king's food. Instead, he asked what King Nebuchadnezzar wanted. He found out that ultimately, the issue wasn't eating the food itself. Daniel suggested an alternate diet that would allow the king to get what he wanted without the Jewish believers having to violate their consciences by eating food that was likely prohibited for them. Daniel applied practical wisdom. He didn't have a kneejerk reaction that would end up making matters worse. When we take gradual steps, we're less likely to burn bridges.

AMBASSADORS FOR CHRIST

All of us—no matter what our role—are ambassadors for Christ. I believe one good way to spread a ministry mentality to everyone in a church is to have at least some leaders who aren't paid for what they do, if that is possible. Rather, they are simply taking ownership of tasks that need to be done because they want to serve Christ and their fellow believers. That's an important kind of modeling that people in the church need to see.

Ultimately, whatever means you use, you want to model what ministry looks like, then give people opportunities to get plugged in. A lot of people aren't sure of what to do. By taking the time to practice what you preach, you give them an opportunity to see what ministry looks like. And you'll see that people are responsive and are willing to get plugged in.

That's the point of Ephesians 4:12, which talks about pastor-teachers "equipping…the saints for the work of ministry." In too many churches, pastors aren't equipping the lay people, who are essential to the life of the church. As you preach what you practice, others will be built up and strengthened so that they, in turn, can equip still others.

LEAVE THE RESULTS UP TO GOD

Recently, someone asked me what encourages me the most about the younger generation in the church. Typically, Christians make negative comments about the youth in their churches. I choose to view them in positive ways and would encourage you to do so as well. They are culturally engaged, they are eager to connect with others, they understand the importance of justice (and we need to steer them toward a biblical view of justice), and many of them are on fire for the gospel.

When I mentioned those traits to a young audience in New Zealand, a young woman came up to me afterward in tears and thanked me. Too often, she had heard criticisms about her generation, which was discouraging. If we want to encourage younger people, we need to commend them for their positive traits. Everything we've discussed in this chapter needs to be done with the next generation in mind.

During an interview, Os Guinness said something I'll never forget. I asked him about his legacy. He said, "Legacy is a secular idea. All that matters is that God says, 'Well done, good and faithful servant.' Our job as leaders is to love the next generation and pass on the faith to them in the same way it was passed on to us." Our job is to be faithful in what we practice *and* in what we preach.

That's what counts. Our job is to watch for opportunities and to act upon them. And the rest we can leave up to God.

CHAPTER 9

LEADERSHIP LESSONS FROM JESUS

Robert Furrow

Jesus is arguably the most influential person who ever lived. His actions and interactions with the people of the first century provide hundreds of lessons on navigating our world and living in a positive and influential manner. Even as I write, high-profile people are embracing cultural Christianity, which values the social and philanthropic aspects of Christianity. Although they reject personal faith in Christ for salvation, they see how Christian principles can affect their lives, community, and world for the better. The influence of Jesus cannot be overstated; He has made the greatest positive impact on the world in the last 2,000 years. Volumes of books could only begin to explore all the ways that Jesus has impacted our world.

The nineteenth-century historian Philip Schaff spoke of the incredible reach and influence of Jesus when he said:

> Jesus of Nazareth, without money and arms, conquered more millions than Alexander the Great, Caesar, Mohammed,

> and Napoleon; without science and learning, he shed more light on things human and divine than all philosophers and scholars combined; without the eloquence of school, he spoke such words of life as were never spoken before or since, and produced effects which lie beyond the reach of orator or poet; without writing a single line, he set more pens in motion, and furnished themes for more sermons, orations, discussions, learned volumes, works of art, and songs of praise than the whole army of great men of ancient and modern times.[1]

Jesus spoke to us directly about leadership through His life and teachings. Over a three-year ministry, He ventured into this realm with His disciples on several occasions, correcting them as to what leadership looks like in the kingdom of God.

If you study the red letters in your Bibles—the words Jesus spoke—you'll find unique teachings about leadership. The application of these lessons is essential for Christian leaders who desire to flourish. We quickly discover that Jesus' leadership style doesn't align with the secular views and principles of leadership. His teachings are distinct because they are not based on human thinking. Rather, they rely on acting in faith, connecting with the living God, and bringing Jesus into our daily lives as we lead others. Through Jesus' example of leadership and His teachings to the disciples, we find a substantial foundation on which to build a biblical kind of leadership.

THE CHURCH'S FIRST LEADERS

The first church leaders were the disciples—the apostles handpicked by Jesus—and they had much to learn. They had not grasped what Christianity would look like, much less how different leadership would be for followers of Christ. Their need for training was evident at the

Last Supper, when Jesus poured out His heart to them about leaving, and they argued about who would become the greatest. What made the situation worse was that they had similar arguments before. Jesus did not rebuke them for their desire to be great. Instead, He redirected them to the radically different concepts of true greatness in the kingdom of God.

THE INVERSION PRINCIPLE

One characteristic most of these lessons have in common is what I call the "inversion principle." This is the concept that the kingdom of God sometimes works in ways that are opposite of the ways of our world. Jesus set an example of the inversion principle when He came from heaven to earth and willingly took a low place to serve humanity. And in serving, He taught us how to lead. Those who continued with Jesus in His trials were promised the privilege of eating and drinking at His table in His kingdom and sitting on thrones judging the 12 tribes of Israel (Matthew 19:28). In the kingdom of God, the human perspective is turned upside down, and it is the least among us who will be the greatest. Jesus said things like, "The last will be first, and the first last" (Matthew 20:16). We are to put other people above ourselves and take the last place. Conversely, the world's leadership philosophy says, "Make yourself known, sell yourself, and get out there in front."

We discover that the inversion principle works because of our faith in God. Instead of trusting in our accomplishments, we need to intentionally seek God's direction, placing our trust in Him and His Word.

THE PATH OF HUMILITY

Humility is a large part of practicing the inversion principle. When we humble ourselves, God shows us His grace and exalts us at the right time: "God resists the proud, but gives grace to the humble. Therefore humble yourselves under the mighty hand of God, that He may exalt you in due time" (1 Peter 5:5-6).

A staff member once asked me about this idea of pride versus humility. He said, "You know, I'm proud of my son when he plays baseball, and I'm proud that I've learned to play the piano." He wondered if these kinds of pride were wrong. But being proud of your child is very different from prideful arrogance. It is okay to feel deep pleasure or satisfaction over achievements or qualities when we turn it into a form of gratitude and give the ultimate credit to God. However, pride in our abilities (or our family's abilities) compared to those of others and believing we are better than others is a dangerous form of pride. To think that we are superior in any way or loved more by God is a hazardous illusion. If we work hard and have a special skill and we think this elevates us above others who have not worked as hard or don't have our ability, then we are displaying arrogance.

The Bible warns us of the danger of a self-glorifying and proud heart: "The Lord detests all the proud at heart. Be sure of this: They will not go unpunished" (Proverbs 16:5 NIV). God promises to honor us when we honor Him with humility: "Humble yourselves in the sight of the Lord, and He will lift you up" (James 4:10).

For this to make sense, we need to have faith in God, believe what He says, and have confidence in the authority of Scripture. Without trust in God's Word, it's entirely impractical to humble ourselves, serve others, and expect to be rewarded. But this is our direction and promise from the Bible. And it is certainly a radically different viewpoint from what we learn in the world.

So, we must examine our hearts, repent from any pride we may find, and ask God to convict us of any pride we don't see. Then, in humility, we must acknowledge that none of our gifts, talents, or skills make us better than anyone else. They are gifts from God to be used for the betterment of His kingdom: "For who makes you differ from another? And what do you have that you did not receive? Now if you did indeed receive it, why do you boast as if you had not received it?" (1 Corinthians 4:7).

What's awesome is that we don't need to have an inwardly boastful attitude about ourselves because our identity, worth, and value have already been given to us by the King of kings and Lord of lords!

Jesus also told us the following:

> When you are invited, go and sit down in the lowest place, so that when he who invited you comes he may say to you, "Friend, go up higher" (Luke 14:10).
>
> He who is least among you all will be great (Luke 9:48).

In Philippians 2:3, we're told, "Let nothing be done through selfish ambition or conceit, but in lowliness of mind, let each esteem others better than himself." That's a serious command for all of us. Do you esteem yourself above others? Notice the verse says, "In lowliness of mind, let each esteem others better than himself." The Greek phrase for "lowliness of mind" is a compound of two Greek words that refer to humbleness of mind.

Verse 4 adds, "Let each of you look out not only for his own interests, but also for the interests of others." This doesn't mean we can't look out for our own interests. Rather, it means that we consider not only ourselves, and we act in ways that show concern for all involved. Also, notice that Philippians 2:3 started with, "Let nothing be done through selfish ambition or conceit." Honest humility is a foundation for developing God-honoring "ambition." Ambition is a key to motivation, and having ambition is not wrong. What we're warned against is a *selfish* ambition that solely considers our own well-being.

In 1988, Christian music artist Michael W. Smith released his fifth album, *i 2 (EYE)*. One of his biggest hits was on this album—"Secret

Ambition." In the song, Jesus challenges the religious leaders who have been seeking their own interests by saying that Jesus' secret ambition was to give Himself away.

The song illustrates that, although selfish ambition is wrong, we can be ambitious about the things of God, such as helping people and encouraging them to grow in their relationship with the Lord. Genuine Christ-centered ambition is promised to be far more rewarding than a life of self-focused ambition. Being humble is a prerequisite for Christian leaders, for only then can we authentically care for others, recognize their needs, and add value to their lives.

There's another Bible passage in which Jesus paints a picture of humility. In Matthew 18:1, the disciples came to Jesus and bluntly asked, "Who then is the greatest in the kingdom of heaven?" Jesus called a little child to Him, set him in the midst of them, and said, "Assuredly, I say to you, unless you are converted and become as little children, you will by no means enter the kingdom of heaven" (verse 3). They wanted to know about who was the greatest, and Jesus basically said, "Why don't you worry about whether or not you're saved? You won't even get into heaven if you aren't like a little child and become converted."

Again, we see the importance of faith. Without the ability to believe and trust as a little child, God cannot complete His work in us. And without faith, we will not follow God's Word.

Finally, in verse 4, Jesus stated the point so it was crystal clear: "Therefore whoever humbles himself as this little child is the greatest in the kingdom of heaven." To achieve greatness, we need to humble ourselves like a little child. This is the inversion principle.

THE WAY OF SUFFERING

You may have heard of the *Via Dolorosa*, a Latin term that translates to "the Way of Suffering." In Jerusalem's Old City, the Way of Suffering is an attempt to recreate the route Jesus took with the cross as He completed the greatest work that has ever been done. What He did at the cross provided the way for all to have access to eternal life and a relationship with God. The picture here is striking, with His intense suffering being part of His greatest work. When we think of being a leader, we generally don't associate it with suffering. I've never heard someone say, "I was inspired to be a leader because of the suffering involved." But would that statement be biblical?

Paul said, "I now rejoice in my sufferings for you" (Colossians 1:24), and "I also count all things loss...that I may know Him and the power of His resurrection, and the fellowship of His sufferings" (Philippians 3:8, 10). Jesus said, "These things I have spoken to you, that in Me you may have peace. In the world you will have tribulation; but be of good cheer, I have overcome the world" (John 16:33). The only promise we have that we'll be free of difficulties and suffering is the promise of heaven. "God will wipe away every tear from their eyes; there shall be no more death, nor sorrow, nor crying. There shall be no more pain, for the former things have passed away" (Revelation 21:4). Until then, we trust that God will use our pain, troubles, and difficulties for His purposes. To God be the glory!

Jesus gave this lesson to the two disciples who, with their mother, asked Him to let them hold the greatest positions of all time. She said, "Grant that these two sons of mine may sit, one on Your right hand and the other on the left, in your kingdom" (Matthew 20:21). You may be thinking, *That's it? That's all she wanted—for her sons to sit at the right and left of the King of glory? That would be a great honor.*

But read Jesus' reply and the disciples' response: "You do not know what you ask. Are you able to drink the cup that I am about to drink, and be baptized with the baptism that I am baptized with?" They said to Him, "We are able" (Matthew 20:22).

Of course they said they were able; they were willing to do anything to have such great positions in the kingdom. Jesus continued: "You will indeed drink My cup, and be baptized with the baptism that I am baptized with; but to sit on My right hand and on My left is not Mine to give, but it is for those for whom it is prepared by My Father" (Matthew 20:23).

Jesus was talking about His suffering on the cross and the suffering that James and John would experience after His death. James was the first apostle martyred; tradition says John was boiled in oil for his faith and somehow survived. John was then exiled to a prison island, where God used him to write the last book of the Bible, the book of Revelation.

Tragically, many Christians today do not appreciate the significance of Christ's suffering at the cross. Crucifixion is arguably the most painful and shameful death ever invented; we get the word *excruciating* from it. Jesus was innocent of His charges; He was plotted against and falsely accused by the religious leaders. He was beaten, mocked, and tortured before they crucified Him. He was betrayed by a friend and denied by another friend. His mother and youngest disciple, John, watched His agony, suffering, and death. This horrific ordeal is how God chose to make the way for anyone to be forgiven by calling on His name, placing their trust in Christ, and receiving eternal life. If God used this immense suffering to bring such glorious salvation, then He could use the suffering of James and John for His good will and purpose. He can also use the suffering we all face, no matter how slight or severe, for His purposes.

James and John did indeed suffer for the great calling of being apostles. There's a way in which all leaders are called to the Way of Suffering. Jesus said, "Whoever desires to save his life will lose it, but whoever loses his life for My sake will find it" (Matthew 16:25). God truly does work in different ways. May our prayer be this: "Lord, as

I endeavor to lead, may You use the hardships and difficulties in my life to do Your work among Your people."

THE GARDENING PRINCIPLE

The Bible uses many illustrations to teach a basic idea I call the "gardening principle."

We will reap what we sow.

> Do not be deceived, God is not mocked; for whatever a man sows, that he will also reap. For he who sows to his flesh will of the flesh reap corruption, but he who sows to the Spirit will of the Spirit reap everlasting life (Galatians 6:7-8).

For some, a favorite scripture for battling sin is Galatians 5:16: "I say then: Walk in the Spirit, and you shall not fulfill the lust of the flesh." Very simply, when we walk in the Spirit, the result is that we won't fulfill the lust of the flesh—whatever sin that might be.

Throughout Scripture, we find other references to the gardening principle that reveal how extensively it impacts our lives.

The mercy we give is the mercy we will receive.

> Blessed are the merciful, for they shall obtain mercy (Matthew 5:7).

The definition of "mercy" here is "withholding deserved punishment." This means we had better be merciful because we all need mercy! I want to be merciful to others so I never have mercy withheld from me. I'd rather hear God say, "Robert, you are full of mercy, and I'm going to be merciful to you."

The way you judge is the way you're going to be judged.

> Judge not, that you be not judged. For with what judgment you judge, you will be judged; and with the measure you use, it will be measured back to you (Matthew 7:1).

Are you a judgmental person? Jesus said that He would judge us by the words we say. "I say to you that for every idle word men may speak, they will give account of it on the day of judgment. For by your words you will be justified, and by your words you will be condemned" (Matthew 12:36-37).

That ought to terrify every pastor because we're also told, "My brethren, let not many of you become teachers, knowing that we shall receive a stricter judgment" (James 3:1). How often do pastors get up and talk about something, and then do those very things?

The Bible says that everyone will be judged, Christians included (see John 5:22-24; 2 Corinthians 5:10; Hebrews 9:27). However, because Jesus already paid the price for sin on the cross, and "whoever believes in Him should not perish but have everlasting life" (John 3:16), the judgment of believers is different—our life's good works will be judged based on our motives and actions. The nonbelievers' judgment will be heartbreaking—they will be eternally cast out of God's presence with no salvation.

According to 1 Corinthians 3:13-14, fire will test each believer's work, of what sort it is—gold, silver, and precious stones, or wood, hay, and straw. If anyone's work endures (gold, silver, precious stones), he will receive a reward; if anyone's work is burned (wood, hay, straw), he will suffer loss when it comes to rewards in heaven.

The way we give affects the way we receive.

> He who sows sparingly will also reap sparingly, and he who sows bountifully will also reap bountifully. So let each

> one give as he purposes in his heart, not grudgingly or of necessity; for God loves a cheerful giver (2 Corinthians 9:6-7).
>
> Give, and it will be given to you: good measure, pressed down, shaken together, and running over will be put into your bosom. For with the same measure that you use, it will be measured back to you (Luke 6:38).
>
> Remember the words of the Lord Jesus, that He said, "It is more blessed to give than to receive" (Acts 20:35).

The way we give—whether sparingly or abundantly, grudgingly or cheerfully—determines how we will receive.

BUT I'M IN CHARGE

If you ever find yourself saying the words, "But I'm in charge," it probably means you aren't. Being in charge is how the world sees leadership. "I want to be in charge, so I'm going to be the boss!" The disciples were upset when they heard that James and John had asked to sit at the right and left hands of Jesus in the kingdom of God.

> When the ten heard it, they began to be greatly displeased with James and John. But Jesus called them to Himself and said to them, "You know that those who are considered rulers over the Gentiles lord it over them, and their great ones exercise authority over them. Yet it shall not be so among you" (Mark 10:41-43).

We are also told in 1 Peter 5:3 not to lord over those entrusted to us. It's good to desire to be a leader (the world certainly needs good leaders!), but we need to remember that we are serving those we lead.

Jesus explained how biblical leaders differ when it comes to the secular notion of "being in charge":

> Whoever desires to become great among you shall be your servant. And whoever of you desires to be first shall be slave of all. For even the Son of Man did not come to be served, but to serve, and to give His life a ransom for many (Mark 10:43-45).

We have all experienced the insecure leader. Because of their insecurity they are mean, bossy, and demanding. (I have had the pleasure of saying "I quit" to a leader like that.)

Quite a few years ago, our church was looking for a facility for our second campus. We had started meeting in a school, and it was time to move on. A church building was for sale a little distance away, so we scheduled an appointment to look at the property. By chance, we met the pastor of the church, and he said he was moving on and the denomination needed to sell the facility. The next day, I called him to ask a few questions. I called him by his name (let's say it was Joe). He said to me, "You will call me Pastor Joe." Immediately I realized what was happening; he was insecure and needed to let me know he was in charge. We ended up not buying the building, but I learned a valuable lesson: It's not attractive when a leader is insecure.

One of the great aspects of being a Christian leader is that we can be confident as leaders because our role is not about ourselves. Remember, we are to do nothing from selfish ambition. Rather, we are to put other people first. As leaders, we are doing what God has called us to do. It's not about us, it's about God. When we realize this, it is easy to put away our insecurities, lean on God, and serve the people around us.

JESUS' EXAMPLE OF SERVING

Foot-washing services have never been my thing. The church I attended when I was 20 had foot-washing services. Men washed men's feet, and women washed women's feet (as it should be). I did not mind washing other people's feet. The process for doing this was straightforward: pick up the feet one at a time, put some soap on a washcloth, scrub the feet, rinse and dry them, and put them down. But for me, the strange part was the way people would wash my feet. First, I preferred that they simply pick them up in a normal way, and not as if they were conducting a holy service. Then they would splash water on my feet, apply some soap, then wash them as if they were afraid they would hurt me. Then they would dry my feet so delicately it seemed they were afraid they might drop and break them. After a couple of these experiences, I knew I wanted no part in such activity.

You might say, "What's the problem? Jesus washed the disciples' feet." Yes, He did—in a culture where foot-washing was an everyday event. It was normal and not part of a special religious ceremony. In those days, people wore open sandals, and their feet got dirty from walking on roads and paths of dirt. That's why it was common for homes to have water by the front door. If you were hosting guests, when they entered, you or a servant would wash their feet as a courtesy.

When Jesus washed the disciples' feet in John 13, He wasn't saying we should have foot-washing services. Rather, He was saying, "As I have taken the role of a servant and washed your feet, I also want you to take the role of a servant and serve one another." Notice what He said:

> When He had washed their feet, taken His garments, and sat down again, He said to them, "Do you know what I have done to you? You call Me Teacher and Lord, and you say well, for so I am. If I then, your Lord and Teacher, have

> washed your feet, you also ought to wash one another's feet. For I have given you an example, that you should do as I have done to you. Most assuredly, I say to you, a servant is not greater than his master; nor is he who is sent greater than he who sent him. If you know these things, blessed are you if you do them" (John 13:12-17).

Do you know when this happened? At the Last Supper, the same event where the disciples were arguing over who was the greatest. I like to think it was at that moment when Jesus got up, girded His waist with a towel, and started to wash their feet. We know Peter got uncomfortable and said, "You shall never wash my feet!" (verse 8). But after a short conversation, Jesus washed Peter's feet as well. What was it that made Peter so uncomfortable? Jesus was the Lord and Master, and in Peter's mind, was not supposed to take the role of a servant. This was the point Jesus was making all along. He wanted the disciples to understand that, as a Christian, being in charge is to be a servant. Jesus, the greatest one who ever lived, gave us an example to serve one another. He gave the disciples a visual lesson of what He had told them earlier—that no one is above serving. When He said, "Do as I have done to you," He did not mean the literal act of washing feet, but rather, being willing to serve others.

The reason Jesus came to earth was to serve us by going to the cross and sacrificing His life so we could live. Paul told us in Galatians 5:13, "You, brethren, have been called to liberty; only do not use liberty as an opportunity for the flesh, but through love serve one another."

EQUIPPING AND ADDING VALUE

As leaders, we must ask ourselves, "What value am I adding? How am I equipping others to be successful?" Because that's the goal. It's not about climbing a ladder, achieving goals for ourselves, or getting that promotion. It's not to achieve accolades for ourselves. The goal is to equip those around us to improve. If our intention is to serve others so they can excel, then our leadership will be incredibly effective. And when people see that we sincerely care about them, their attitude will shift positively toward us, which can definitely enhance a working relationship.

Leadership is different in Christianity. The greatest ways we can apply what we learn from Jesus is to humble ourselves, seek wisdom from God, and serve others. We must come to grips with this and be able to say, "God, it doesn't matter whether I'm praised or promoted or how You use me. I just want to do Your will. I want to minister to the people You called me to lead. I want to be faithful to You. And when I'm exalted, I want it to be for Your glory." As 1 Corinthians 10:31 says, "Whatever you do, do all to the glory of God."

There is no good work that God calls you to for which the Word of God will not equip you. God's Word gives us strength (Psalm 119:28), wisdom, and understanding (Proverbs 2:1, 9). If we're not applying the principles we find in Scripture, we will be ineffective leaders. But God will bless us when we apply His Word to our leadership roles.

Remember that Jesus' leadership lessons are unique because faith is an essential element to them. You've got to place your full trust in God. In every aspect of leadership, Jesus plugs God into the equation. Many of us have benefited from using corporate leadership techniques in the church. But faith is required to understand, execute, and obtain the greatest success with Jesus' principles.

May God help us to evaluate our leadership—our goals and methods, and the ways we treat the people around us. May we be eager to incorporate biblical principles into our leadership so that we will experience the blessings God has promised to those who hear His Word and do it. This is Jesus' example: He did not come to be served but to serve, and we should do the same.

CHAPTER 10

AN UNDIVIDED HEART: INTEGRITY IN LEADERSHIP

Lenya Heitzig

Teach me your way, Lord, that I may rely on your faithfulness;
give me an undivided heart, that I may fear your name.
I will praise you, O Lord my God, with all my heart;
I will glorify your name forever.

PSALM 86:11-12 NIV

A boneyard of broken lives lies in the wake of public figures whose values proved duplicitous and who have been exposed as sex offenders, financial embezzlers, or worse. Political, famous, or religious—these once-shining stars have become fallen angels in dramatic, disastrous ways. Each exposure leaves shocked, disbelieving followers and fans wavering in their faith.

A *Sports Illustrated* article wrote of an illustrious athlete who cited a well-known quote: "Fame is vapor, popularity is an accident, and money takes wings. The only thing that endures is character."[1] That sports star? O.J. Simpson. He heard the quote one night while watching TV and said he never forgot it. Sadly, he didn't actualize it, either.

In today's culture, we find a puzzling disconnect between what people say and what they actually do. It is most tragic when it comes to leaders in the faith. We want them to be "doers of the word, and not hearers only" (James 1:22). Often, these men and women profess to know God, but their actions betray their beliefs. They fail to practice what they preach.

Ravi Zacharias soared as one of the foremost apologists of his day. He launched the largest apologetic ministry in the world. He authored dozens of best-selling books. He traveled worldwide as a highly sought-after speaker. He acquired several commercial properties both foreign and domestic. But his legacy crumbled because of secret sin. He is said to have sexually abused countless women during massages in more than a decade of ministry, was accused of rape, and had hundreds of pornographic photos in his possession just months before his death in 2020 at age 74.

- Ravi Zacharias International Ministries, the largest apologetic ministry in the world, stopped doing apologetics.
- His wife resigned from the ministry.[2]
- Many of his books are no longer being printed.[3]
- Christians around the world devastatingly lost their trust in him.
- Unbelievers everywhere found reason to distrust Christians and Christianity.

We long for leaders with *integrity*. The Bible extols leaders and gave a special designation to the kings that did "what was right in the eyes of the LORD" (1 Kings 22:43). When Israel was a divided kingdom, the Judean kingdom consisted of two tribes in the south that had 20 kings in their long history. Just eight of those were offered that beautiful epitaph. Sadly, it seems there are more compromised leaders than committed ones.

In Solomon's book of Proverbs, the person of integrity is contrasted to the fraud:

- "Whoever walks in integrity walks securely, but whoever takes crooked paths will be found out" (10:9 NIV).
- "The integrity of the upright guides them, but the unfaithful are destroyed by their duplicity" (11:3 NIV).
- "The righteousness of the upright delivers them, but the unfaithful are trapped by evil desires" (11:6 NIV).

Integrity describes a Christlike life that is both consistent and honest—a person who is honorable and decent. This person is incorruptible because of their strong moral principles. Those who possess these qualities live without deception or pretense. These attributes become the backbone of a person's character, highlighting their upright lives. People with integrity have nothing to hide because they are the same in private as they are in public. They are integrated in all aspects of their personalities.

Rick Ezell wrote,

> Integrity is not reputation—others' opinion of us. Integrity is not success—our accomplishments. Integrity embodies the sum total of our being and our actions. Integrity is not something we have, but something we are. It inevitably shows itself in what we do and say. Integrity is needed because people are watching us. Will our behavior match our beliefs? Will our character correspond with our confession?[4]

Strip everything in your life away. If your name, reputation, and character remain, you've lost nothing of value.

Integrity is derived from the root word *integer*, meaning whole. In mathematics, whole numbers are called integers. Engineers design structural integrity into bridges, airplanes, and buildings. Otherwise, tragedy—like the collapse of the beachfront condominium Champlain Towers South in Surfside, Florida—strikes. That disaster resulted in the deaths of 98 people.

I like the picture that integer conveys of being whole because it feels more powerful, poetic even. Everybody is seeking to be made whole—no missing pieces, no broken parts. David's prayer for an undivided heart beautifully captures the idea of integrity in leadership. It inspires us to become people who are intact, complete, and consistent.

We've established what integrity is, but how do we develop it in our lives? Just like the old hymn "One Day at a Time" reminds us, we must take life day by day. Jesus said, "Do not worry about tomorrow, for tomorrow will worry about its own things. Sufficient for the day is its own trouble" (Matthew 6:34).

Rome wasn't built in a day, and neither is your character. We must live each day, each decision, and every thought like they are building blocks. Paul admonished, "So then, just as you received Christ Jesus as Lord, continue to live your lives in him, rooted and built up in him, strengthened in the faith" (Colossians 2:6-7 NIV).

Our lives are constructed decision by decision, act by act, and thought by thought. Today matters. Moment-to-moment obedience matters. Faithfulness today builds great marriages, strong ministries, and an amazing legacy. A person with integrity chooses to do the right thing all the time.

Billy Graham said, "Our world today is looking for men and women with integrity, for communicators who back up their ministry with their lives. Our preaching emerges out of what we are. We are called to be holy people—separated from the moral evils of the world."[5]

Name a few people of integrity you know. For Christians, Billy Graham rockets to the top of that list. My husband and I have enjoyed a long friendship with Billy's son Franklin Graham. And because of that friendship, we've had the privilege of observing the Billy Graham Evangelistic Association from behind the scenes, and we were able to meet with Billy and his wife, Ruth, and their kids, on many occasions.

In 1948, a winsome 31-year-old Billy Graham was lauded as a successful evangelist. He had three charismatic men by his side as he entered a ministry that would last six decades: George Beverly Shea, Grady Wilson, and Cliff Barrows.

After a series of successful meetings in Modesto, California, these men challenged one another to compile a list of the greatest pitfalls that men in ministry face. Surprisingly, those lists were strikingly similar. To guard against allegations of abuse of money, sex, and power, these men took bold steps to avoid the slightest hint of scandal. Although they never created a written document, they committed to four core principles. Cliff Barrows eventually dubbed this pivotal pact the Modesto Manifesto, which included these resolutions:

- Never handle money alone.
- Never criticize local churches.
- Never exaggerate about crowd size.
- Never be alone with any woman other than their wives.

As of 2013, Graham appeared 57 times in the top ten on Gallup's annual "most admired" people list.[6] This recognition was due in no small part to his reputation for sexual fidelity—a reputation guaranteed by the most famous provision of the Modesto Manifesto.

Skip and I have followed these boundaries to the best of our abilities. Last year, a medical student stayed in our house for a month while working on her residency. She was married, God-fearing, and a pastor's kid. Midway through her stay, I had to leave town for a family emergency. Skip and I agreed that he would stay in a hotel until I returned—not because of temptation, but to keep his reputation, the reputation of the church, and God's reputation free from reproach.

If I have a meeting with a man, I always leave my office door ajar or have an assistant join the meeting. This reminds me of Romans 14:16: "Do not let your good be spoken of as evil." We never want to give people a reason to make false assumptions or to gossip.

I will be forever humbled for having a "fly on the wall" opportunity to witness Chuck Smith's ministry at Calvary Chapel Costa Mesa. He, too, was a man of integrity. Pastor Chuck Smith possessed a 1,000-watt smile that ran from ear to ear. A tanned, outdoorsy guy, he exuded that all-American surfer vibe. His expository teaching through the Bible—chapter by chapter and verse by verse—gave my faith a strong foundation because the Word of God does the work of God in the people of God.

Chuck taught Skip and me about financial accountability, which was key in his life and ministry. He was frugal and faithful with God's resources. Because he was a good steward in the small things, God trusted Pastor Chuck with much. I remember when someone gave him an avocado orchard. One night, he brought boxes of avocados to share with us after the Sunday evening service. It's remarkable all that God added to his ministry.

Those of us who were the first generation to plant churches from Calvary Chapel Costa Mesa have compiled a list of "Chuck-isms"—the phrases he repeatedly shared with us. One of the best is "Where God guides, God always provides." God is not broke. He owns "the cattle on a thousand hills" (Psalm 50:10). As ministry leaders, we don't need to worry about our finances *if* we're following God's guidance. When Skip and I moved to New Mexico, we never asked for donors or partners. We both got jobs because we believed that if God was calling us, He would provide for us.

Chuck, in his commentary on 2 Corinthians 9–10, said, "I have always been disturbed over the emphasis that churches so often place upon giving. And that is why I, perhaps, [have] gone the other direction in the pendulum and say so little about giving. That is why we never mention to you any needs that might exist, because we're not looking to you; we're looking to the Lord to supply for the work of the ministry. And when God guides, God always provides."[7]

Skip took that idea a step further when we launched Calvary Church. We did not take a formal offering by passing the plate. We simply set up a box in the foyer for people to give as God guided them. When a local pastor came to check out our service, he warned Skip that the church was doomed to failure. We would never survive without cajoling people to give. Needless to say, through 40 years of ministry, our church has never lacked resources.

Another adage Chuck often said from the pulpit is that if anyone had given money to the church and regretted it, they could go to the accounting office for a refund. I've heard Skip repeat the same sentiment. Paul said, "Let each one give as he purposes in his heart, not grudgingly or of necessity; for God loves a cheerful giver. And God is able to make all grace abound toward you, that you, always having all sufficiency in all things, may have an abundance for every good work" (2 Corinthians 9:7-8).

Chuck affirmed that God does not want

> your gift to be by pressure. Someone really putting the pressure on you, you know. Everybody's looking now to see what you're going to give. And God doesn't want the gift to come by necessity, by constraint, by pressure. But what you give to God, which God receives and accepts, is that which you give with just a cheerful heart. Giving hilariously...It's a joy to be able to give. And only that should you really give to God. That which is given hilariously, because it is only that which God really respects and honors.[8]

Finally, my husband has taught me about being a cohesive, authentic human being. He is completely integrated in all he does, everywhere he goes. He doesn't do pretense or performance. He's shown me how to be the same person behind closed doors as the person on the speaking platform. I watch him rise early each day to read his Bible and pray. When I have the opportunity to address our congregation, I remind them that their pastor is the same godly man at home. They can trust him.

When it comes to finances, Skip has instituted an annual outside audit of the church, adding credibility to his stewardship of God's money. This protects the church's finances from being squandered or extorted.

I want to close with a list of characteristics that a person of integrity displays:

1. A person of integrity keeps their promises.
2. A person of integrity tells the truth.
3. A person of integrity admits when they are wrong.
4. A person of integrity respects others.
5. A person of integrity is trustworthy.
6. A person of integrity pursues justice and fairness.
7. A person of integrity lives humbly.
8. A person of integrity does not compromise their core values.
9. A person of integrity gives others credit.
10. A person of integrity forgives others.

If you look at this list and feel like it's daunting and you don't measure up, you're in good company. We all feel that way at times. Perhaps you've fallen short in some way—don't give up. Growth in integrity is a journey, and God calls us to continue to run the race of faith with endurance.

Remember that integrity is gained thought by thought, act by act, and day by day. God knows our frames—He knows that we are but dust. He's in the business of turning our worst failures into our greatest victories. He promises "to give them beauty for ashes, the oil of joy for mourning, the garment of praise for the spirit of heaviness; that they may be called trees of righteousness, the planting of the Lord, that He may be glorified" (Isaiah 61:3).

CHAPTER 11

HOW TO LEAD PEOPLE TO THE TRUTH OF CHRISTIANITY

Frank Turek

The Son of Man did not come to be served,
but to serve, and to give his life as a ransom for many.

MARK 10:45

When you try to lead a friend or relative to follow Jesus, do you ever feel like you're pushing a rope? No matter what you do, they are unmoved, apathetic, and sometimes even hostile to Christianity.

I often experience that kind of attitude during my "I Don't Have Enough Faith to Be an Atheist" presentations on college campuses. When atheists or people from another faith express any hostility during the question-and-answer session, I'll usually ask them this question: "If Christianity were true, would you become a Christian?"

I've had atheists stand at a microphone in front of hundreds of people and say, "No!"

No? I'll then ask, "How is that reasonable? Why would you *not* believe something that turned out to be true?"

Their rejection reveals it's not a matter of the head but the heart. They're not on a truth quest but a happiness quest. They don't want the God of the Bible to exist because *they* want to be God over their own lives. They want moral freedom and will believe whatever will get them that, even if the evidence for God and Jesus is strong.

Prominent atheists have admitted this:

- Professor Thomas Nagel, a philosopher at New York University, wrote, "I want atheism to be true and am made uneasy by the fact that some of the most intelligent and well-informed people I know are religious believers. It isn't just that I don't believe in God and, naturally, hope that I'm right in my belief. It's that I hope there is no God! I don't want there to be a God; I don't want the universe to be like that. My guess is that this cosmic authority problem is not a rare condition and that it is responsible for much of the scientism and reductionism of our time."[1]
- That same cosmic authority problem seemed to infect the late Christopher Hitchens, a brilliant British atheist I debated twice several years ago. He rebelled against the very thought of God, describing God as a "cosmic North Korean dictator" peering into our sex lives. Hitchens claimed that he was refusing to live under the "tyranny of a divine dictatorship." Even his book title screamed out contempt—*god Is Not Great: How Religion Poisons Everything*. While Christopher was undeniably brilliant and verbally gifted, his book was short on evidence and long on attitude. Which is why I concluded both of my debates with Christopher this way: "You can sum up Christopher's book in one sentence: There is no God, and I hate him."[2]

- Theoretical physicist Lawrence Krauss describes himself as "an anti-theist, like my friend Christopher Hitchens was."[3] That's someone who not only doesn't believe in God but doesn't want there to be a God.
- Oxford chemist Peter Atkins, who has debated several Christian scholars, was asked what evidence would convince him that Christianity was true. He admitted that nothing would convince him. "But what if Jesus appeared to you?" asked moderator Justin Brierley at one of his debates. Atkins said he wouldn't believe it and chalk it up to "madness."[4]

Now, I am not saying this is the case for all atheists. Nor am I saying that an atheist's motivation proves that atheism is false—someone can have the wrong motives and still be right. What I am saying is that many atheists don't want Christianity to be true.

To prove this is the case for people in general, I ask audiences to think of a non-Christian friend or relative whom they have tried to persuade to become Christian but, so far, that person has given negative responses. So that I can walk you through this exercise I do with audiences, take a moment now to think of a non-Christian you know personally.

Got someone?

Okay, here's my question: Is the person you're thinking of on a relentless pursuit of truth—that is, do they earnestly want to know whether Christianity is true, or are they apathetic or hostile to Christianity? When I ask that question, 99 percent of my audiences (sometimes 100 percent!) say that the person they are thinking of is apathetic or hostile. The truth is, most people are looking for God like a criminal is looking for a cop! They are running from Him and running toward what they think is "happiness" (see Romans 1:18-32).

What's the main problem with the "happiness" approach? You *can* make yourself "happy" over the short term by living for yourself—by following whatever whim or desire is on your heart. But over the long term, you're headed for disaster. If you're living only for yourself, how are you going to be able to maintain stable and mutually satisfying relationships? Who wants to live with a "me monster" for long? Who will put up with you? And if others do manage to put up with you, it's unlikely the relationship will be very satisfying for either party.

It's not just loss of relationships that will be a problem. If you follow your every impulse on your "happiness" quest, you'll also risk addiction, job loss, debt, sickness, and premature death, not to mention an eternity in torment away from the ultimate source of happiness. Nevertheless, some people would rather continue down that "me monster" road because, as Solomon put it, "Hell and Destruction are never full; so the eyes of man are never satisfied" (Proverbs 27:20).

This is a critical insight for leaders of any kind. We need to realize that people don't always make decisions that line up with reason or the truth. People are more inclined to act on incentives rather than truth.[5] Those incentives normally have something to do with sex, money, or power—as the apostle John put it, "the lust of the flesh, the lust of the eyes, and the pride of life" (1 John 2:16). In fact, as Paul wrote in Romans 1, people often suppress the truth to get what they want. They know that God exists because creation, design, and morality are effects that point back to a divine creator and designer who is moral. But some people don't like the moral implications of that kind of being, who they think will take away what they really want. So they suppress the truth to go their own way. The real issue is not the existence of God but their *resistance* to God.

THREE FUNDAMENTALS OF LEADERSHIP

Resistance creates a challenge for leaders because you need to account for more than just facts. If you want people to follow you, you can't just speak to their minds but must also speak to their emotions and will. As Blaise Pascal put it, "People almost invariably arrive at their beliefs not on the basis of proof but on the basis of what they find attractive." Christianity can be a hard sell because most people don't find denying yourself attractive. On the other hand, the person of Christ, who sacrificed Himself to save us (see Mark 10:45), is enormously attractive.

So, what does this mean for leading Christians? A leader must recognize that our minds, emotions, and wills contribute to every decision we make. That's why direction, trust, and desire—which address a follower's mind, emotions, and will respectively—are three of the most important fundamentals of leadership. For people to follow you consistently, they must know where you're going (direction), trust you to help them get there, and have a desire to go in the direction you're going.

Let's start with the first fundamental of leadership, which is direction. (I'm going to spend most of this chapter on direction, but I'll also provide some ideas on how you can earn trust and build desire.) If you're not going in a particular direction, how can you lead anyone? Without direction, you may end up leading people to accept the status quo, and not really lead them anywhere.

The direction I want to lead people is toward Jesus—not the Jesus we may have invented in our minds, but the Jesus of the Bible who lived a perfect life, took the punishment due us upon Himself on the cross, and rose from the dead to prove He is God. The primary way I try to lead people to Christ is through evidence. I want to make a case for the facts that God really exists, Jesus predicted and accomplished His own resurrection from the dead, and the Bible is the Word of God and can be trusted as the guide for life. Following Peter's command to "always be prepared to give a defense to everyone who asks you a reason for the hope that is in you" (1 Peter 3:15), let's see how you can make a clear and memorable case for Christianity.

THE CASE FOR CHRISTIANITY IN FOUR QUESTIONS

As I mentioned above, the facts alone may not be enough to convince someone to become a Christian. But the facts are still important. What you win people *with*, you win them *to*. If you win someone to accept Christ through emotion alone, you can lose them to emotion alone. But if you win people with facts, their faith can withstand any emotional changes they experience because facts never change.

You can find a detailed case for Christianity in 12 sequential points laid out in the book I did with Norman Geisler, *I Don't Have Enough Faith to Be an Atheist*.[6] However, I often make an abbreviated case to church and college audiences because as leaders, I believe we should keep our presentations as simple and memorable as possible.

These are the four questions we need to investigate to see whether Christianity is true:

1. Does truth exist?
2. Does God exist?
3. Are miracles possible?
4. Is the New Testament true (especially about the resurrection of Jesus)?

If the answer to those four questions is yes, then basic Christianity—or *Mere Christianity*, as C.S. Lewis put it in one of his book titles—is true. If the answer to any of those questions is no, then Christianity is false. Let me now share the abbreviated case for Christianity.

THE ABBREVIATED CASE FOR CHRISTIANITY

Question 1: Does truth exist?

It's common to hear people in our postmodern culture say things like, "There is no truth." Or, "You've got your truth; I've got my truth." Or, "All truth is relative."

When someone says, "There is no truth," you should ask that person, "Is *that* true? Is it true that there's no truth?" In other words, those who claim there is no truth are implying it's *true* that there is no truth! But this is a self-defeating statement. It's like saying, "I can't speak a word of English." That's a self-defeating claim because you're using English to say it.

Self-defeating claims violate the self-evident law of logic known as the law of noncontradiction, which states that opposite ideas cannot both be true at the same time and in the same sense. You can detect self-defeating claims by simply turning the claims on themselves and asking a question. Here are a few more examples:

> All truth is relative. *Is that relative truth?*
>
> There are no absolutes. *Is that an absolute?*
>
> There isn't *the* truth, only my truth. *Is that just your truth or the truth?*
>
> You can't know anything. *Then how do you know that?*
>
> You should be skeptical of everything. *Should I be skeptical of that?*
>
> You should not judge. *Isn't that a judgment? Why are you judging me for judging?*

Ultimately, it is absurd to say there is no truth. If there were no truth, then you would never go to school, read a book, draw a scientific conclusion, convict someone of a crime, or be able to catch someone in a lie. All those things presuppose truth.

It's undeniable that truth exists. To deny it is to affirm it. That leads us to ask: Is it objectively true that God exists?

Question 2: Does God exist?

Outside of communicating with us directly, God shows that He exists through two primary means: through His Word, and through His works. Because the apologetic task is to show that the Bible is God's Word—not assume it—let's start with God's works. God reveals Himself by what He has created or done. This includes creation, design, and the human conscience. You don't need the Bible to know that some kind of God is behind these works, and the apostle Paul said as much in Romans chapters 1 and 2.

To say that God reveals Himself by His works is to say that we know God by His effects. We see effects, such as creation, design, and the conscience and, like scientists, we reason from effect back to cause. Who is the cause behind creation, design, and the conscience? We can answer that question by looking at these three important effects that need to be explained:

1. The Beginning of the Universe

Today, even atheists are admitting that this universe is an effect. In other words, it had a beginning—space-time and matter literally came into existence out of nothing. As the late Stephen Hawking put it, "Almost everyone now believes that the universe, and time itself, had a beginning at the big bang."[7]

The only question is, what could have caused space-time and matter to come into existence out of nothing? Atheists can cite no natural cause inside of space-time and matter. Instead, the cause must transcend space-time and matter. In other words, the cause appears to be spaceless, timeless, immaterial, powerful enough to create the universe out of nothing, personal enough to choose to create, and intelligent enough to be able to make a choice.

2. The Fine-Tuning of the Universe

In recent decades, we've discovered that our universe is fine-tuned with extreme precision. If any one of a number of attributes were slightly different about our universe, either the universe wouldn't exist at all, or it couldn't support life. For example, if the gravitational force were different by 1 part in 10^{40} compared to the strong nuclear force, we wouldn't exist. That's 1 part in 1 with 40 zeroes following it!

To grasp that level of precision, imagine stacking dimes on the entire North American continent to the moon (that's more than 238,000 miles). Do the same on a billion more North American continents. Mark one dime red, mix all those huge piles of dimes together, blindfold a friend, throw him on that one humungous pile, and ask him to pick just one dime randomly. The chance of him picking that one red dime is 1 in 10^{40}. And that's just one of about a dozen similarly precise numbers related to the laws of nature. If any one of them were different, we wouldn't exist. This level of precision is beyond the reach of chance and demands a designer.

3. The Moral Law

We have an effect inside of us that causes us to believe we have certain moral obligations and rights. As the Declaration of Independence explains, these rights are "self-evident" and come from our "Creator."

Without our Creator, there would be no objective moral law or standard beyond ourselves. Therefore, we couldn't justify why the Nazis were wrong and the Allies were right. Unless God exists, the question of whether the Holocaust was wrong is just a matter of human opinion. But because we know the Holocaust was wrong regardless of human opinion, there must be a moral lawgiver whom we are obligated to obey. That moral law is an effect that comes from God.

The cause behind these three effects must have at least these seven attributes: *spaceless, timeless, immaterial, powerful, personal, intelligent,* and *moral.* Now, when you think about these attributes, who do you think of? God, of course. Because the cause is personal and intelligent, it can't be a *what*—it must be a *who*. This is the being beyond the universe who created the universe.

However, this evidence alone isn't enough to establish Christianity. The First Cause could be some other theistic or deistic God with those same attributes. To see whether the Creator of the universe is the God of the Bible, we must answer the next two questions.

Question 3: Are miracles possible?

Christians are mocked at every turn for believing in the virgin birth, Jonah and the great fish, the resurrection, and many other miracles. Yet these miracles are easy to believe if the greatest miracle in the Bible truly has occurred.

What's the greatest miracle in the Bible? The one the atheists are admitting the evidence for: the creation of the universe out of nothing! If Genesis 1:1 is true, then every other miracle in the Bible is at least possible. Now, atheists don't think God created the universe. But, as we just saw, the cause of all nature must transcend nature. That cause has some of the same attributes of what Christians call God.

And it's not just Christians who believe in miracles—everyone believes in at least one miracle. Atheists believe that *no one* created the universe out of nothing. That takes more faith to believe than believing *someone* created the universe out of nothing. In fact, for atheism to be true, every single miracle claim and spiritual experience in the history of the world has to be mistaken! Is that possible? Yes. Is it reasonable to believe? No.

Despite the fact we are living in a miracle (the universe), some people remain skeptical because they haven't personally witnessed a miracle and thus have trouble believing in the resurrection. But why should they expect to see a miracle? If miracles like resurrections occurred routinely, then the resurrection of Christ would lose the very rarity that makes it a special act of God designed to get our attention. That is, miracles must be rare if they are going to have their desired effect.

In the Bible, God uses miracles to confirm a message from Him. Contrary to popular belief, God did miracles through people rather infrequently in the Bible. They were done during the three periods when God was confirming new revelation—during the lives of Moses, Elijah and Elisha, and Jesus and the apostles. Why should we believe those people? Because God did miracles through them to confirm the messages He communicated through them. We might say that the sign confirms the sermon; the miracle confirms the message.

Now, imagine if miracles happened all the time, and you said to an unbeliever, "Jesus Christ rose from the dead to prove He is God, so trust in Him for eternal life!" If the unbeliever responded by saying, "So what? My Uncle George just rose from the dead two weeks ago. Why shouldn't I trust in him?," what are you going to say? For the resurrection of Christ to be convincing, resurrections must be extremely rare events. Demanding rare, special acts of God to be regular occurrences is to demand that miracles not be miracles and would defeat the very purpose of a miracle!

Because we know the Bible's greatest miracle has already occurred—the creation of the universe out of nothing—let's see if the rare, predicted special act of God called the resurrection occurred as well. If it did, then we will know that Christianity is true. If it didn't, then we will know that Christianity is false (as the apostle Paul himself said in 1 Corinthians 15:14).

Question 4: Is the New Testament historically reliable (especially about the resurrection)?

The reason we believe in Christianity is because a pivotal event known as the resurrection occurred. Christianity is not true because a group of documents we now call the New Testament say it's true. In fact, Christianity would be true if the Bible never existed! How so? Because Christianity did not originate with a book; Christianity originated with an event—the resurrection of Jesus of Nazareth.

Do you realize there were already thousands of Christians before a single line of the New Testament was ever written? Why? Because Jewish believers in Yahweh said they witnessed a resurrected Jesus.

But how do we know that these Jewish believers in Yahweh didn't just make up a story? How do we know that the documents they wrote—which testify of the resurrection—are historically reliable?

In the book *I Don't Have Enough Faith to Be an Atheist*, we have a chapter titled "The Top Ten Reasons We Know the New Testament Writers Told the Truth." We don't have the space to cover all ten here, but let me briefly mention two of those reasons.

Embarrassing Details

One reason we know that the New Testament writers were not inventing a new religion is because their testimonies included many embarrassing details. This trades on the obvious point that people usually don't lie to make themselves look bad. We may lie to make ourselves look good, but we won't lie to embarrass ourselves. Here are just a few of the embarrassing details admitted by the New Testament writers:

- The disciples depict themselves as dimwits. They are slow to understand Jesus and His mission, and didn't really "get it" until after He ascended to heaven.
- Their leader, Peter, is called "Satan" by Jesus and then denies Christ three times after saying he never would.
- The disciples run away in fear when Jesus is crucified, while the women are the brave ones who stay at the cross.
- Then the women—whose testimonies, in those days, were not considered as credible as those of men—discover the empty tomb and the resurrected Jesus while the men are hiding for "fear of the Jews" (John 20:19).

All four Gospels say the women are the first witnesses (one of them formerly demon-possessed!), when it would have been far more convincing to people in that culture if the men were the first witnesses.

- After Jesus is resurrected, while giving the Great Commission, we read this about the 11 disciples: "some worshiped him; but some doubted" (Matthew 28:17). Who would ever make up that they doubted the risen Lord?

Jesus is also depicted in embarrassing ways:

- He is a called "a drunkard" (Luke 7:34) and accused of being demon-possessed (Mark 3:20-27). Certainly not flattering.
- His family says He is "out of his mind" (Mark 3:20-21), and His own brothers didn't believe in Him (John 7:5).
- Jesus' feet are wiped with the hair of a prostitute (Luke 7:37-39), and there are two prostitutes in His bloodline (Tamar and Rahab, Matthew 1:3, 5). Who would invent and insert prostitutes into the Messiah's genealogy? (Can you imagine a historian in Egypt writing that the Pharoah was the product of prostitutes? "Off with your head!")
- Jesus seems not to know when He is coming back (Matthew 24:36). Isn't He supposed to be God? Then how can He not know when He is coming back?
- Jesus cries out on the cross, "My God, My God, why have You forsaken Me?" (Matthew 27:46).

There are very good explanations for why these seemingly embarrassing details about the disciples and Jesus are true and not problematic.

What *isn't* a good explanation is that the New Testament writers simply made them up.

Excruciating Deaths

We have very good evidence from the first century that many of the apostles were tortured and martyred for declaring that Jesus rose from the dead.[8] This raises a couple of questions for those who say the story about the resurrection was invented.

First, why would the Jewish writers of the New Testament documents say that a man claimed to be God and rose from the dead if it didn't happen? They already believed that they were God's chosen people and had no motive for making up a new religion. Prior to Jesus, they didn't believe two core aspects of the Christian story were even possible: a man could claim to be God (that would be blasphemy and the very reason Jesus was executed), and that one man would rise from the dead before the final resurrection. Yet that's exactly what they said happened.

Second, they had nothing to gain and everything to lose by inventing the resurrection story. They didn't get what normally motivates people to invent things—sex, money, or power. In fact, they got quite the opposite. They were thrown out of the temple and then beaten, tortured, and killed—certainly not a list of perks! Why didn't they simply recant and save themselves if they invented the story? They not only had no motive to invent a resurrected Jesus, they had every motive to say the resurrection did *not* happen.

The best explanation of the facts is that the New Testament writers didn't create the resurrection—rather, the resurrection created the New Testament writers. There would have been no New Testament written by Jews in the first century if there had been no resurrection. They also filled their documents with eyewitness details that agree with those provided by non-Christian writers and archaeology, as well as details that show they were independently witnessing the same events.

The bottom line is that when you take a fair look at the evidence, the New Testament documents appear to be historically reliable. You don't have to prove they are inerrant to show that Christianity is true, just that they are a generally reliable record of what Jesus said and did.

How much faith does that take? From a Christian perspective, faith means trusting in what you have good evidence to believe. But according to atheist Richard Dawkins, faith means blindly believing something that is even against the evidence. Using that atheist definition, I would say it takes more faith to believe the resurrection did *not* occur than to believe it did.

Because Jesus predicted and accomplished His own resurrection from the dead, it's clear He is God. Whatever God teaches is true. If you go further into the evidence, you'll see we have good reason to believe that Jesus taught the Old Testament is the Word of God and He promised the New Testament. Therefore, we can establish, on the authority of Jesus, that the Bible is the Word of God.[9]

WHAT IF A PERSON WON'T LISTEN TO REASON?

What if you make a sound case for Christianity and the person you are speaking to is still unmoved? Then that person might have a trust or desire issue. That's why you should always ask the question, "If Christianity were true, would you become a Christian?"

If the person hesitates or says no, he or she has a trust or desire issue. More evidence isn't the solution because evidence isn't the problem—they are.

What can you do for such people? There are at least five ways you can respond to them.

First, you can pray for them. Pray that God will soften their hearts and give them eyes to see the truth. Not only do the Scriptures tell us to pray, but I've seen and heard of many cases where long-term prayer led to conversions.

Second, you can love them. Love doesn't mean you approve of everything they do; love means you seek what's best for them according to God's will. And that will require you to tactfully *disapprove* of their evil behaviors precisely because you do love them and want to protect them from evil. As Paul wrote in the chapter that so many people read at their wedding but few obey, "Love does not delight in evil but rejoices with the truth. It always protects, always trusts, always hopes, always perseveres" (1 Corinthians 13:6-7 NIV).

Third, you can ask questions rather than make statements. Questions get people thinking and do not require you to be an expert. You are asking them to justify what *they* believe, which means you don't need to make a case for anything—they do.

Greg Koukl's book *Tactics*[10] will help you do this. The first two questions Greg equips you to ask are "What do you mean by that?" and "How did you come to that conclusion?" For example, if someone says, "I can't believe the Bible because it's been changed over the centuries," don't give a dissertation about why they are wrong. Instead, ask them for proof they are right. You will find that most people don't have a coherent worldview that they've thought through. Instead, they've heard incorrect slogans and statements about Christianity, but when asked to defend their opinion, aren't able to do so. When someone throws a challenge at you, ask them for clarification with Greg's first question and for evidence with Greg's second question.

Fourth, you can plant seeds that, when sprouted, will show that their worldview has problems, or that Christianity is the right worldview. This is important because before someone is going to consider converting to your worldview, they usually need to doubt their worldview first.

Perhaps their opposition to Christianity is because of all the hypocrisy and evil they've seen done by so-called Christians. They may even think that the bad behavior of some Christians disproves Christianity altogether.

You can and should agree with them that such behavior is a stain on Christians. But here again, questions are your friend. Ask them: Does a Christian's bad behavior mean that Christianity itself is false? Does it mean that God doesn't exist, or Jesus didn't rise from the dead? Does bad behavior by atheists show that atheism is false? No. Instead, it shows that we all have a problem called sin—a problem that Jesus came to fix for us.

Author John Dickson, in his excellent book *Bullies and Saints*,[11] asks people who have been wronged by Christians to consider this question: "When someone plays Bach poorly, who do you blame?"

You don't blame Bach! Likewise, when someone plays Jesus poorly, you don't blame Jesus. I know this might be a news flash to the non-Christian world, but Christianity is not Christians—Christianity is Jesus! If someone wants to know about Christianity, he or she needs to keep their eyes on Jesus. He is the Savior, substitute, and example. The rest of us fall short. And that's to be expected. If we were perfect, we wouldn't need a Savior!

Yes, I know, I'm still giving reasons when it's a trust or desire issue. But it's better to be reasonable than unreasonable. After you acknowledge a non-Christian's hurt, there comes a time when it's appropriate to plant seeds. One seed you can plant is Dickson's question.

You might also agree there are times when you're a hypocrite as well. In fact, everyone is. No one lives perfectly even to their own standards, atheists included.

In one of my debates with Christopher Hitchens, he went on and on about the evil religious people have done. I agreed with him. I said religious people have done evil. "But you're proving our worldview, Christopher. We are evil and need a Savior." I admitted that I'm a hypocrite and can't live up to the standard that Jesus exhibited. But if I could, I wouldn't need Him. So when someone tells me they can't become a Christian because there are too many hypocrites in church, I always say, "Please come; we have room for one more!"

The church is a hospital for sinners. It's not a country club for saints. To say I can't go to church because there are too many hypocrites is like saying, "I can't go to the gym because there are too many out-of-shape people there." That's one reason they are at the gym!

Finally, after doing all that, the fifth way you can respond to someone who doesn't want Christianity to be true is to wait. Yes, wait. Why should you expect everyone to agree with you right now? You shouldn't. I'm 62 years old at the time of this writing. When I was 22, I didn't agree with my 62-year-old self. So why should I expect everyone to agree with me right now? I shouldn't.

But if we are praying, loving, asking questions, and planting seeds, it might be that over time the people we love or care about will eventually become Christians. Sometimes that happens after a tragic event. They are moved to reach out because they are looking for hope or for answers. And if you've done the first four things—praying, loving, asking questions, and planting seeds—your phone is going to ring, and that person is going to be on the other end. When the student is ready, he will summon the teacher.

USING YOUR TIME WELL

Because there is excellent evidence that truth exists, God exists, miracles are possible, and Jesus rose from the dead, you can show beyond a reasonable doubt that the basics of Christianity are true. But even when you, as a leader, provide this clear direction, you will discover that some people will reject your message on emotional or volitional grounds. Those objections involving trust and desire are difficult to overcome, which will leave you feeling as though you're pushing a rope. That's why you should ask, "If Christianity were true, would you become a Christian?" If they hesitate or say no, they have desires that incentivize them to say no. So pray, love, ask questions, plant seeds, wait, and leave the results to God.

But even if you are a fantastic servant leader who makes a great case for Christianity and you employ all of those suggestions, the people you're trying to reach may remain obstinate and never become Christians. At some point it may be wiser for you to "shake the dust off your feet" (Matthew 10:14) and spend your limited time with those who are more open to what you have to say. You can't bring everyone you lead to Christ, but you can bring Christ to everyone you lead.

PART 2

QUESTIONS AND ANSWERS

CHAPTER 12

QUESTIONS AND ANSWERS ABOUT BIBLICAL LEADERSHIP

The chapters in this book are taken primarily from messages that were spoken at a conference on leadership, which was hosted by Calvary Chapel Tucson. For the benefit of those who attended, a question-and-answer session was held during the conference. A select portion of that session is provided here, with some adaptations. Questions were received from the audience, and Adam Parsons, who is on staff at Calvary Chapel Tucson, served as the moderator, posing the questions to the participating conference speakers.

Adam Parsons: How should church leaders navigate politics in their churches?

Gary Hamrick: Because we are believers in Christ, and because everything we do—not only in ministry but in life—should be done through the lens of the Bible, we shouldn't make politics off-limits. We should let the Bible inform us on how we view everything, including politics. And we have to realize the Bible addresses politics. In the Old Testament, prophets repeatedly spoke truth to power to various kings. Usually they issued rebukes, and they didn't avoid talking about a king's actions or his political policies. In the New Testament, Jesus told His listeners they were to render to Caesar what belonged to Caesar (Matthew 22:21).

Church leaders often avoid bringing up political matters for two reasons. One, because they are afraid of losing their tax-exempt status. And two, because they are afraid of losing people who help to support the church.

But there should never be a reason to avoid saying what needs to be said. It is God who builds the church, and church leaders are entrusted with the responsibility of teaching and speaking the truth.

At our church, we haven't shied away from politics. When candidates share the same biblical worldview that we do, we're willing to invite them up on the platform and introduce them.

Some years ago, someone asked me if I ever preached election sermons. I asked, "What's an election sermon?" He showed me a two-volume set of books comprised of sermons that pastors preached during the colonial era and America's first 150 years. These pastors would speak in their pulpits about candidates and issues, and based on biblical criteria, they would alert their congregations about how they ought to vote. These pastors were unashamed, and America's values were shaped because these pastors were a flame for what is righteous.

Today, however, there are many who won't address political issues. But we have to realize that these days, so much of politics is tied to issues that are moral in nature, and the Bible has much to say about what is right and what isn't. When we refuse to address politics, we're refusing to address moral issues, yet biblical leaders are obligated to lead their people on moral issues. After all, we're to be salt and light in the world.

So, until Jesus comes, we should do our duty to help people understand which policies are righteous or unrighteous, and which people stand behind those policies. And then let the people in the church make their decisions accordingly.

There are lessons we can learn from history too. The church was largely silent in Europe during the 1930s and 1940s, and church leaders were reluctant to speak against Nazi Germany. Dietrich Bonhoeffer, who said, "God means for the church to be the conscience of the state," was one of the few who stood up to Nazi Germany. It cost him his life. He was executed in April 1945 at the age of 39.

We cannot be silent when we see evil encroaching on our culture. The church is meant to be a restraining force against evil in the world. There's coming a day when the church will be raptured, and evil will suddenly fill the vacuum. But until that day, we should stand strong and be God's voice in a dark world.

David Guzik: I believe Christians should be more politically engaged rather than less, and they should be biblically informed because so many political policies today have to do with moral issues. By avoiding politics, we end up letting non-Christians dictate morality for the culture. For us to stay out of politics is a wrong approach. We have been given a stewardship in our democracy, and we should take advantage of it.

At the same time, Christians should not put their hope in politics or politicians. While we should do all we can to make our communities better in the name of the Lord, we should do so without putting our hope in politics or in politicians.

Daniel Fusco: I like to remind people that Jesus wasn't political in the traditional sense. Jesus was neither partisan nor apolitical. Jesus was subversively political—so much so that His opponents, who normally disagreed with each other, got together to crucify Him. Jesus came to teach us a more excellent way, and He blazed a unique trial for us to follow. As believers, we know that Jesus is our Savior and Lord. He is God's anointed, and He alone deserves our allegiance. I believe one of the biggest mistakes the body of Christ makes with politics is that we accept the playing field as it is laid out for us by the world. Instead, we should follow Jesus and His subversive political stance.

As Christians, we desire to allow God's kingdom to come and His will to be done on Earth as it is in heaven. To do that, we must not accept the lie that Jesus perfectly aligns with the partisan political climate we live in. Instead, the children of God should be leading ahead with the politics of Jesus, relating to the world as Jesus did. We have to ask ourselves: Are we politically subversive like Jesus, or are we just accepting what politicians or political parties are pushing? For many of us, the political voices in our newsfeed are so loud that we cannot hear the still, small voice of Jesus telling us there is a more excellent way.

Robert Furrow: Obviously the purpose of the church is not to get someone elected. We know what the purpose of the church is. As Paul said in 1 Corinthians 2:1-2, "When I came to you, brothers, [I] did not come with excellence of speech or of wisdom declaring to you the testimony of God. For I determined not to know anything among you except Jesus Christ and Him crucified." The purpose of the church has always been to proclaim the gospel of Jesus Christ because that is the power of God to salvation, not politics (Romans 1:16).

Yet because so much of politics deals with moral issues, we need to engage with those issues. Which means venturing into the realm of politics. If we become afraid of getting involved with politics, then we will end up acquiescing important issues to the world. For example, when there is a state bill that allows for abortions up until birth, we don't want to be silent. We need to speak up, go to the polls, and vote for people who think the way we do so we can stop such bills from becoming law. Otherwise, we're doing nothing to prevent what is morally wrong.

If we as believers are silent, we will end up becoming like the churches that didn't speak up against Nazi Germany. So many of the issues today are weighty with regard to moral issues, so as Christians, we need to get involved. But at the same time, we need to keep our focus on proclaiming the gospel that saves people.

Jim Gallagher: Historically, as Christianity spread the message of the gospel, it led to change. That was true about ancient Rome, and it's true about when Europe began to realize a need to stop the slave trade. As believers addressed the atrocities of slavery, change came about.

That kind of change starts with the message of the gospel. As people are set free and their lives change, they see what's wrong within the culture, and they say, "No, this is not okay. How can we address this?" We live under a unique kind of government that allows us to speak up and to vote for what we believe is right. We can also respond when governments overreach their boundaries, as happened during COVID season.

During COVID, churches responded in two ways. Some stood against the overreach of the government and said, "This is not okay." Others pointed to Romans 13 and said, "We need to obey the law of the land." The point here is that we have a political system that allows citizens to speak their voice. So we should be willing to get involved with politics, and that might even mean the Lord wants us to take on a role in our local government.

Robert Furrow: I have a good friend who, for many years, has worked at a crisis pregnancy center. She is actively involved in getting churches to talk about abortion, which is considered a political issue. Yet many churches aren't willing to talk about abortion from the pulpit. And for us as Christians to be silent when it comes to life-or-death issues is unfathomable. Issues like abortion are of eternal consequence. So it doesn't make sense to say, "That issue is political; I'm avoiding it."

Adam Parsons: Given that we live in a culture that seeks instant gratification, what are some ways that we can guide the next generation of believers to understand the importance of taking the long view when it comes to growing in their relationship with Jesus?

Ed Taylor: I think too many leaders in the church don't emphasize the fruit of the Spirit enough, and encouraging believers to cultivate that fruit requires long-term discipleship. Self-control and self-denial take time to develop. And they're necessary for teaching believers to say no to instant gratification.

Also, all generations of believers need to have love, joy, peace, patience, kindness, goodness, faithfulness, gentleness, and self-control flow out of their lives (Galatians 5:22-23), not just the next generation. We all need to help each other to be actively walking in the Spirit, and that's an ongoing process that requires long-term involvement in each other's lives. Ministry leaders need to do that, too, because, as 1 Peter 5:2 says, we're to "shepherd the flock of God which is among you."

Also, we can't teach others to avoid instant gratification if we haven't dealt with that problem in our own lives. We need to look at ourselves first before we try to teach others how to grow in their relationships with Jesus and deny self. Only then can we look someone else in the eyes and say, "What God has done in me, He can do in you."

Adam Parsons: What does unifying with others in the gospel mean? Can you unify with someone with whom you disagree on issues such as egalitarianism, evolution, inerrancy, differences in eschatology, and so on?

David Guzik: If you are talking about nonessential issues—issues that do not pertain to whether or not a person is a brother or sister in Christ—then I certainly hope so.

Of course, it's important for us to agree on the core beliefs of the faith, such as Jesus being the Son of God, Him being the Messiah, believing that His sacrificial death paid for our sins, that salvation is by grace alone. We cannot compromise on those.

But then there are secondary or tertiary issues that have no bearing on our salvation. And if we disagree on those, because we are brothers and sisters in Christ, and because we're in the same family, we need to find a way to get along, to love and respect one another.

It's good for us to have a vision for what God wants to do in the broader body of Christ. Though we may disagree on some things, still, we are brothers and sisters in Christ, and our common ground is the gospel.

That doesn't mean we should avoid talking about our areas of disagreement. When we do talk, we should do so with a good spirit that says, "I'm not going to treat you like an enemy." Now, even if another person is an enemy, Jesus said we are to love our enemies (Matthew 5:44). But how much more should we love those who are part of God's family!

What's amazing is how we can meet with believers from completely different cultures, backgrounds, economic classes, and have other major differences, yet feel the most incredible kinship with them—all because we are united in Christ. We want to do what we can to preserve that.

Jim Gallagher: In Scripture, we read about how Paul and Barnabas had a disagreement. This disagreement created a division that ultimately led to the creation of two different missionary teams (Acts 15:36-41). Barnabas and Mark went to Cyprus, and Paul and Silas went through Syria and Cilicia. The ideal here was that all four of them continued to do the work of proclaiming the gospel.

When you look at what Acts 15 says about the disagreement, you can't say that one or the other team was right or wrong. They had a disagreement over nonessential differences, but they didn't let it affect their service for the Lord, and it didn't prevent them from working together in the future.

In Ephesians 4:3, Paul urged us to "keep the unity of the Spirit in the bond of peace." The essentials unite us—Jesus has already made that possible. But we need to endeavor to be at peace with one another. We may have differences of opinion, but we should still love one another in the midst of that, and we don't want to divide over the nonessentials.

Daniel Fusco: God's plan has always been for unity within diversity. It is that way within the Trinity, and the apostle Paul showed us that it is that way within the church as well. To be a bit more practical, unity is often context-driven. The unity that is needed among those on a church's leadership team calls for a greater level of theological and stylistic unity. There may be other situations where unity can be experienced when there is a lot more diversity of opinion.

At Crossroads, where I have the pleasure of being one of the pastors, we have activities where we are willing to work together with people we might disagree with because we want to partner, in the name of Jesus, with others to care for our community. For example, in our outreach to foster kids, we're willing to work with anyone who has a heart of care for those kids. That can include working with people who are not yet believers.

I realize that everyone draws these lines in different places, and I also think that that is good. Some leaders may disagree with what another leader chooses to do, but let us remember that before the Master, a servant stands or falls. So our disagreements don't need to be reasons for division. It is my sincere hope that there is less divisiveness in the body of Christ overall. I love to remind people that God's grace unites where people's flesh divides.

Robert Furrow: As we talk about this kind of unity, we need to distinguish between actual differences of opinion and heresy. It's possible for someone to differ on an issue with us and not be a heretic. Just because you disagree with someone on an issue doesn't mean that person is a false teacher. It depends on the issue at hand.

Ed Taylor: Ultimately, we should be more focused on looking for more ministry opportunities in our communities, and not so much on people we can or can't partner with. We do want to be careful, but not to the point that ministry becomes paralyzed. Then we end up not doing anything, or doing very little for the Lord. We want to let the Lord use us in great ways.

Adam Parsons: I've got a question here from a pastor who has a family and serves in a small church. He and his family are wearing all the hats to keep the church running, and the pastor also has another job so he can support the family. How can he lead well and keep going, even when he's working so hard and getting discouraged? How can he and his family keep God's purpose and perspective?

Jim Gallagher: That was the situation my wife and I found ourselves in. We left a larger church and moved to Florida to help a small group of people who needed someone to shepherd them. At the time, our oldest son was five, we had identical twins who were three, and we had a six-week-old child.

We didn't know anyone at this new church. I prepared the Sunday messages, wrote the children's ministry program, and tried to lead the worship. My wife and I did everything, and one thing that helped us to persevere was remembering that we were in this together.

Also, before we left our larger church, many of our friends were praying for us, and they continued to pray heroic prayers of faith. I'm sure that helped. But through this, I learned that God was discipling all of us in our family. He was using our situation to perfect us, to perfect our family relationships, to develop our spiritual giftedness and calling. It was helpful to realize God was using our circumstances to make us what He wanted us to be.

We should also be careful not to let other people's expectations of us affect us and our families. Some people will have unrealistic expectations. They may have good intentions, but a leader will know what's best for themselves and their own family.

Above all, realize that whatever situation you are in, it's part of what God has allowed because of what He wants to accomplish in you, your spouse, and your children. And it's preparing you for whatever future ministry He has for you.

Robert Furrow: As leaders, many of us will find ourselves in seasons of great sacrifice. Serving is hard work, and it's rare to not have problems. But God will not give you more than you can handle—I really believe that. He will help you get through your season of struggle. Yes, it may be difficult, but God will give you what you need.

Jim Gallagher: In a season of sacrifice, God is not calling you to sacrifice your children on the altar of ministry. Absolutely not. One of the most vivid accounts in the Old Testament is the story of Abraham taking Isaac up Mount Mariah. This happened in the context of a culture in which human sacrifices took place. Through this, God made it clear that He Himself would provide a substitutionary sacrifice and not require that Isaac be sacrificed. God was also making a powerful statement against human sacrifices. And when it came to dealing with sin, He would provide a substitutionary sacrifice.

I say all that to point out that caring for our families is vital. God has entrusted them to us, and children shouldn't suffer because of our work in ministry. We need to be careful.

Daniel Fusco: Whether the church or organization is established or young, whether it's small or large, we have to constantly look at what we are doing and ask: Has God actually called me to do this? Is this effective? Is this the best use of whatever time and energy I have? The struggle that is so real for every leader is that all the things that we can do are usually good things. But there are a limited number of resources. So I subscribe to the "do few things but do them well" mentality.

We need to make sure that we don't just work in the ministry, but we always work on the ministry. That always involves essentializing what we do. There are things that have been used powerfully, but their season has passed, and they should be retired. Or they may still be effective, but the available energy and resources need to be used in a different area. You can always bring them back at a later date if the situation changes. But when a leader and their family is stretched out so far that there is exhaustion or discouragement, it's time to reassess what is being done and why. It is time to make hard decisions and create space for the Lord to do the new things He wants to do.

Adam Parsons: Robert and Sean, both of you spend time fielding questions from people on YouTube. Why is apologetics so essential? And have you noticed changes in the kinds of apologetics questions people are asking, especially over the last ten years?

Robert Furrow: We are now approaching 40 years of ministry as a church. About a decade or so ago, I realized a need to communicate, from the pulpit, how we can defend the Christian faith. So I've been intentional about including apologetics in my sermons. And in the church, we've created content for apologetics issues that we are introducing to all those who are part of Sunday school from children to young adults.

We're doing this because we want to help our younger people so that when they encounter challenges to the faith—maybe at school—they will know how to answer. For example, a teacher or professor might claim there are many contradictions in the Bible. We're equipping our people so they know how to answer that allegation. We teach in Sunday school classes about how we got our Bible, and how the fact there are so many ancient manuscripts gives us the assurance the Bible is reliable and can be trusted. And we explain that the so-called contradictions have excellent explanations behind them that disprove the claims that the Bible has contradictions.

Sean McDowell: There are timeless truths and timeless questions, and there are timely truths and timely questions. Timeless questions are the ones people will always ask: Is Jesus God? Is the Bible true? Did Jesus rise from the grave?

Because people are always asking these questions, it's good to equip ourselves to know how to answer them. These core questions will never go away.

But then there are questions of the day, questions that change because of what's happening around us. In 1972, my dad wrote *Evidence That Demands a Verdict*, a book that deals with apologetics. We updated the book in 2017, and now there are three new chapters just on the topic of knowledge and truth alone. Why? Because the way people approach and think about truth has shifted so much. People are saying, "That may be true for you, but it's not true for me." We've seen a shift from truth being objective and real and discoverable by all, to it being internal and subjective and changing from person to person. I believe it's going to get worse as we use artificial intelligence more. We're going to find it more difficult to tell what is true and what isn't.

Because the way people think is changing so much, we need more wisdom and discernment than ever before. And we need more love for truth than we've ever had. That's just one shift we're seeing.

Another is that people are more hurt and broken than ever. We're seeing increases in mental illness, anxiety, and depression. A person's hurts can affect the way they process truth.

Still another area is that culture has shifted a lot on moral issues. For example, views about same-sex marriage have changed significantly in a short period of time. So where we stand on moral issues is becoming a more pressing matter than it has been in the past.

We are also seeing a renewed interest in God and the supernatural. The days of the New Atheists—who called the Bible anti-science and grossly immoral and said that we'd be better off without it—are gone. Many new influencers are strikingly open to the Christian story. In fact, many thinkers now claim that America and Western civilization need Christianity so they can survive and flourish. The God-conversation has shifted.

Those are some of the shifts we've seen. And because the culture continues to change, it's vital for us to keep up with how to defend Christianity. We need to know what God's Word says. Only then can we effectively take a stand when people ask us questions. We need to know what we believe so that we will know what to say.

ABOUT THE CONTRIBUTORS

Robert L. Furrow established Calvary Tucson in 1985 and serves as lead pastor. His teachings are shared on various platforms, including CalvaryTucson.com, YouTube, TV, and radio, and his *Truth Quest* podcast authentically discusses Bible questions. Other ministries include hosting the Calvary Chapel Southwest Pastors and Leaders Conference since the early 2000s and providing support globally to those in need through the Practical Christian Living Foundation, which he cofounded.

Daniel Fusco is the lead pastor at Crossroads Community Church in Vancouver, Washington. Many people start their day with his #2MinuteMessage on his Facebook page, and he hosts the *Real. with Daniel Fusco* TV show as well as *Jesus is Real* on radio. He is the author of multiple books, including *You're Gonna Make It: Unlocking Resilience When Life Is a Mess.*

Jim Gallagher has been the pastor of Calvary Chapel Vero Beach (Florida) since 1998. Jim is the Bible teacher on *Step by Step* on Calvary Radio and is the author of *Hearing His Voice: Discovering the Will of God* and *Always: A Handbook on Marriage.* Jim's devotional blogs through every chapter of the Bible are available at https://pjimgallagher.com/.

David Guzik is a teaching pastor at Calvary Chapel of Santa Barbara and has been in Christian service for more than 40 years, including seven years as a missionary in Germany. He is known for his online commentary on the Bible, and his teaching can be found at enduringword.com. He also has a daily podcast, *Enduring Words with David Guzik*.

Gary Hamrick is the pastor of Cornerstone Chapel in Leesburg, Virginia, home to several thousand weekly worshippers both in person and online across the country and around the globe. Gary is also on the board of directors for the Museum of the Bible and the Family Research Council, both in Washington, DC.

Lenya Heitzig has a heart for reaching out to hurting people through tangible acts of love. She is the founder of Reload Love, a ministry which touches the lives of children affected by terrorism. Lenya also serves as the executive director of *She.ol.o.gie* Ministry at Calvary Church, pastored by her husband, Skip.

Skip Heitzig ministers as senior pastor of Calvary Church to more than 12,000 people weekly. He is the author of many books, including *The Bible from 30,000 Feet*, and holds a DD and PhD from Trinity Southwest University. *Connect with Skip*, his popular multimedia teaching ministry, includes video, audio, and online resources.

Sean McDowell (PhD) is the author of numerous books, including *End the Stalemate*. As an associate professor in Biola University's Christian Apologetics program, an internationally recognized speaker, and the host of a popular Christian apologetics YouTube channel, Sean is committed to exploring the biggest questions about God, morality, and contemporary culture.

Ed Taylor is the pastor of Calvary Church in Aurora, Colorado, and has been in ministry for nearly 35 years. He teaches nationwide on the *Abounding Grace* radio broadcast and hosts a podcast program on leadership, called Lead2Serve. He is the author *Letting Go of Your Past* and *God's Help for the Troubled Heart.*

Frank Turek is the founder and president of CrossExamined.org, an apologetics ministry, and he speaks more than 100 times a year, frequently to youth and college students. He is an award-winning author or coauthor of several books, including *I Don't Have Enough Faith to Be an Atheist* (coauthored with Norman L. Geisler). He hosts a weekly TV program and an apologetics podcast.

NOTES

CHAPTER 2—WHAT IS A GREAT LEADER?

1. Adapted from John C. Maxwell, *Everyone Communicates, Few Connect: What the Most Effective People Do Differently* (New York: HarperCollins Leadership, 2010), 205.

2. Abraham Lincoln Online, "Failures," *Abraham Lincoln Online*, 2018, http://www.abrahamlincolnonline.org/lincoln/education/failures.htm, accessed February 16, 2024.

3. This is the opening line of Charles Dickens's novel *A Tale of Two Cities*.

4. Warren Wiersbe, *Be Strong (Joshua): Putting God's Power to Work in Your Life* (Colorado Springs, CO: David C. Cook, 2010), 30.

5. David M. Atkinson, *Leadership–by the Book* (Dyer: Grace and Glory Publishing, 2007), 58.

6. Flavius Josephus, "Chapter 8" in *Antiquities of the Jews: Book VI*, trans. William Whiston (Urbana, IL: Project Gutenberg), https://gutenberg.org/files/2848/2848-h/2848-h.htm#link62HCH0008. Accessed February 16, 2024.

7. Charles Spurgeon, "Stewards," *The Charles Spurgeon Sermon Collection*, https://www.thekingdomcollective.com/spurgeon/sermon/3350. Accessed April 17, 2024.

8. Kevin Halloran, "Christian Ministry Burnout: Prevention, Signs, Statistics, and Recovery," *Word Partners*, January 20, 2020, https://wordpartners.org/resources/christian-ministry-burnout-prevention-signs-statistics-and-recovery. Accessed February 16, 2024.

9. Adapted from Charles R Swindoll, "Children," in *The Tale of the Tardy Oxcart* (Nashville, TN: Thomas Nelson, 1998), 72.

10. Abigail Van Buren, "Letter 3 of 4," *Dear Abby*, November 9, 2003, https://www.uexpress.com/life/dearabby/2003/11/09.

CHAPTER 3—KEYS TO EFFECTIVE LEADERSHIP FROM NEHEMIAH

1. Oswald Chambers, *My Utmost for His Highest: An Updated Edition in Today's Language,* ed. James Reimann (Grand Rapids, MI: Discovery House, 1992).

CHAPTER 5—THE SUFFERING LEADER

1. David Guzik, "Study Guide for 2 Corinthians 11," *Blue Letter Bible*, https://www.blueletterbible.org/comm/guzik_david/study-guide/2-corinthians/2-corinthians-11.cfm. Accessed April 18, 2024.
2. In English, the Greek word is typically spelled *hypomone*. But because that's a transliteration of the Greek characters and it's pronounced *hupomone*, I chose to use the spelling *hupomone*.
3. Jeff Robinson, "Spurgeon on Suffering and the Pastoral Ministry," *Founders Ministries*, https://founders.org/articles/spurgeon-on-suffering-and-the-pastoral-ministry/. Accessed April 18, 2024.
4. Jon Courson, *Courson's Application Commentary*, 3 vols. (Nashville, TN: Thomas Nelson, 2004), Olive Tree Bible Software, 2 Corinthians 12:9(a).

CHAPTER 6—LEADING IN CRISES: TWO NECESSARY QUALITIES

1. Bob Smietana, "For some pastors, the past year was too much to bear," *AP News*, May 7, 2021, https://apnews.com/article/health-coronavirus-pandemic-religion-8a91c31370ffeaf8cc4d93e53e088835.
2. Meagan Gillmore, "Younger Pastors Took the Brunt of the COVID-19 Burden," *Christianity Today*, November 6, 2023, https://www.christianitytoday.com/news/2023/november/covid-study-pandemic-churches-younger-ministers-quit-health.html.
3. C.H. Spurgeon, *Lectures to My Students* (Grand Rapids, MI: Zondervan, 1954), 321-355.
4. Spurgeon, *Lectures to My Students*, 321.
5. Christopher Hibbert, *Nelson: A Personal History* (Cambridge, MA: Perseus Books, 1996), 261.
6. Spurgeon, *Lectures to My Students*, 327.
7. Spurgeon, *Lectures to My Students*, 328.

CHAPTER 7—LEADING AS YOU FOLLOW

1. Saint Augustine, *The Confessions of Saint Augustine* (Grand Rapids, MI: Revell, 2005), 16-17.

CHAPTER 8—LEADING BY BUILDING RELATIONAL BRIDGES

1. Bob Tiede, *340 Questions Jesus Asked* (Cru, Leadingwithquestions.com, 2024), vii.
2. Andy Bannister, "Learning Questions from the Master," in Bob Tiede, *340 Questions Jesus Asked*, 97-98.
3. *A New Kind of Apologist*, gen. ed. Sean McDowell (Eugene, OR: Harvest House, 2016).
4. Gregory Koukl, *Tactics: A Game Plan for Discussing Your Christian Convictions*, 10th anniversary edition (Grand Rapids, MI: Zondervan Reflective, 2009, 2019), 46.

CHAPTER 9—LEADERSHIP LESSONS FROM JESUS

1. Philip Schaff, *The Person of Christ* (New York: Charles Scribner's Sons, 1881), 29-30.

CHAPTER 10—AN UNDIVIDED HEART: INTEGRITY IN LEADERSHIP

1. Paul Zimmerman, "All Dressed Up, Nowhere to Go," *Sports Illustrated Vault*, November 26, 1979, https://vault.si.com/vault/1979/11/26/oj-simpson-retires-49ers-nfl.
2. Daniel Silliman and Kate Shellnutt, "Ravi Zacharias Hid Hundreds of Pictures of Women, Abuse During Massages, and a Rape Allegation," *Christianity Today*, February 11, 2021, https://www.christianitytoday.com/news/2021/february/ravi-zacharias-rzim-investigation-sexual-abuse-sexting-rape.html.
3. Kate Shellnutt, "Ravi Zacharias's Books Pulled by HarperCollins After RZIM Investigative Report," *Christianity Today*, February 12, 2021, https://www.christianitytoday.com/news/2021/february/ravi-zacharias-books-harper-collins-lee-strobel-rzim-report.html.
4. Rick Ezell, "Are You a Person of Integrity?," *Lifeway*, January 1, 2014, https://www.lifeway.com/en/articles/parenting-teens-are-you-a-person-of-integrity.
5. Billy Graham, "10 Quotes from Billy Graham on Integrity," *The Billy Graham Library*, February 13, 2021, https://billygrahamlibrary.org/blog-10-quotes-from-billy-graham-on-integrity/.
6. Kristy Etheridge, "Billy Graham Named Among Gallup's 'Most Admired' for 57th Time," *Billy Graham Evangelistic Association*, December 30, 2013, https://billygraham.org/story/billy-graham-named-among-gallups-most-admired-for-57th-time/.
7. Chuck Smith, "Verse by Verse Study on 2 Corinthians 9–10 (C2000)," *Blue Letter Bible*, https://www.blueletterbible.org/Comm/smith_chuck/c2000_2Cr/2Cr_009.cfm. Accessed July 22, 2024.
8. Chuck Smith, "Verse by Verse Study on 2 Corinthians 9–10 (C2000)."

CHAPTER 11—HOW TO LEAD PEOPLE TO THE TRUTH OF CHRISTIANITY

1. Thomas Nagel, *The Last Word* (New York: Oxford University Press, 1996), 130.
2. You can see both of those debates on the Cross Examined YouTube channel.
3. Lawrence Krauss, *A Universe from Nothing: Why There Is Something Rather than Nothing* (New York: Atria Books, Kindle edition, 2012).
4. Justin Brierley, "The 'God' of the 'Philosophers,'" *Religion & Liberty*, vol. 34, no. 3, July 8, 2024, https://www.acton.org/religion-liberty/volume-34-number-3/god-philosophers.
5. Why don't more Christians take a bolder stand for Christ in our decaying culture? Because they are incentivized to keep quiet. They don't want to lose their jobs or put tension in their relationships with loved ones who are embracing sinful lifestyles.

6. Norman L. Geisler and Frank Turek, *I Don't Have Enough Faith to Be an Atheist* (Wheaton, IL: Crossway, 2004).

7. Stephen Hawking and Roger Penrose, *The Nature of Space and Time*, The Isaac Newton Institute Series of Lectures (Princeton, NJ: Princeton University Press, 1996), 20.

8. See Dr. Sean McDowell, *The Fate of the Apostles* (New York: Routledge, 2018).

9. For more on that and the evidence for Christianity, see the book I coauthored with Dr. Norman Geisler, *I Don't Have Enough Faith to Be an Atheist*, and my subsequent work, *Stealing from God: Why Atheists Need God to Make their Case.*

10. Greg Koukl, *Tactics: A Game Plan for Discussing Your Christian Convictions* (Grand Rapids, MI: Zondervan, 2019).

11. John Dickson, *Bullies and Saints* (Grand Rapids, MI: Zondervan, 2021).

HARVEST HOUSE PUBLISHERS
EUGENE, OREGON